Estuary Fishing:
Afloat & Ashore

Estuary Fishing: Afloat & Ashore

Dave Lewis

Illustrations by Anne Maclean

BLANDFORD

*This book is dedicated to my wife Alison
and two young children, Amy and Luke.
Always a tremendous support.
Always willing to let Dad disappear on 'just
one more fishing trip'.*

A Blandford Book

First published in the UK 1995 by Blandford,
a Cassell imprint
Wellington House, 125 Strand, London WC2R OBB

Distributed in the United States by Sterling Publishing Co. Inc
387 Park Avenue South, New York, NY 10016–8810

Distributed in Australia by Capricorn Link (Australia) Pty Ltd
2/13 Carrington Road, Castle Hill, NSW 2154

British Library Cataloguing-in-Publication Data
A catalogue record for this book is
available from the British Library

ISBN 0 7137 2536 2

Typeset by Keystroke, Jacaranda Lodge, Wolverhampton

Printed and bound in Great Britain by
Hillman Printers (Frome) Ltd

Previous pages
The peat ledges at Redwick in South Wales.
Note the distinct gullies. At high tide, when
anglers are forced to retreat and fish off the sea
wall, this is where the fish will be searching for
food. Always ensure that you do not get cut
off by a flooding tide or fall off the edge
of the ledge, especially at night.

Contents

Foreword

Mel Russ

Editor, *Sea Angler* and *Boat Angler* magazines.
Consultant editor, *Improve your Sea Angling*.

Anglers old and new will enjoy and learn a lot from this information-packed book because it is written from the heart by an angler who has a passion for his sport.

In 30 years of journalism I have yet to find anybody who is fired up with so much enthusiasm. I wouldn't say he lived for his sea angling but he would have a severe bout of depression if he couldn't mix with anglers, pit his wits against the fish and take a picture or two along the way.

But there is always one thing that tempers his fishing, and that is safety. Unlike many foolhardy sea anglers, Dave never, ever takes risks. And I hope those who buy this book read his clear messages of safety on and by the sea and follow them to the letter.

The sea is one of the most powerful forces on the planet and rarely gives you a second chance. The oceans, including what seems to be a placid estuary, is certainly not the place to horse around.

I personally owe Dave a couple of big 'thank you's'. He is a regular contributor to all three sea angling magazines that I work on. His professionalism, constant stream of ideas, his catch sense and knowledge of tackle is second to none and has helped to make all three titles leaders in their field.

John Wilson, TV's Mr Angling, displays a sea trout caught trolling. Always check local by-laws and obtain the necessary licences before you fish for sea trout.

You can send Dave off anywhere, from Portugal to the north of Denmark, and he always returns with an informative story supported with some great photographs.

Like all angling writers, he has to have a go himself even when working, and often finds himself in front of the camera. It happened a couple of seasons ago when he hooked the biggest ling ever taken off the Danish coast.

The really big thank you is for saving my neck during a day's dinghy fishing in Ireland's Shannon estuary. Dave was on one boat, I was on another, drifting for pollack close to a sheer cliff face.

Our boat developed engine trouble and was in danger of being smashed up against the rocks. Despite being some distance away, Dave spotted our plight and came steaming down to us at full throttle. Assessing the situation in seconds he soon had a tow rope rousted out and pulled us out of danger. So, thanks Dave, for saving the boat, the crew and my neck!

I suppose this message should be the theme of any authoritative angling book: enjoy your fishing to the full, use the best bait, fish the best marks, learn how to use your tackle and above all be a safe and responsible sea angler.

Knowing Dave as I do, all these key factors will be skilfully worked into his first ever book. Enjoy it, practise what he tells you, catch a lot of fish and live to tell the tale!

Introduction

The countless estuaries around the British coastline provide the angler with some of the best sea fishing available today. Whereas fishless sessions are all too often a feature of open beaches and many rock marks, the majority of our estuaries pay host to sizeable populations of fish, albeit at different times of the year.

The water within many estuaries is usually heavily coloured with sand and silt, constantly held in suspension by the continual scouring action and movement of the tide and river currents. This dirty water will very often result in catches made during daylight that equal or even exceed those taken at night from open beaches, especially when the water is very shallow.

Although only relatively few species of fish are truly at home in the brackish water conditions found within most estuaries, many 'true sea fish' can be caught at certain times. This is more so in the case of the larger estuaries although, even then, results are very often entirely dependent on the state of tide and other seasonal factors, such as the amounts of local rainfall or whether snow on distant mountain ranges is thawing – and, increasingly today, on the amount of pollutants and other noxious substances that ultimately get washed into the estuary from rivers.

During prolonged periods of hot sultry weather, many inshore marks in the open sea become stagnant, and fishing them can be a virtual waste of time, with fish moving out into deeper water where conditions are far more favourable. But within an estuary, with the tide flushing the area during its twice daily cycle, the fishing can be very good.

Unlike most areas of the open foreshore, access to fish is not always so freely available within, and in the vicinity of, estuaries. The National Rivers Authority exercises a considerable amount of control within most estuaries, with the level of their jurisdiction extending for some six miles out to sea.

Anglers wishing to fish in some estuaries will require an NRA rod licence which covers them to fish for freshwater coarse fish and eels. Local tackle shops or the NRA office will be able to advise on the exact areas where a rod licence is a requirement. In most instances, these areas are realistically defined so as not to prevent sea anglers gaining free access to fish. When required, the cost of a freshwater fish and eel rod licence is minimal but be warned, fines for infringements are hefty.

Many areas within estuaries are privately owned with access and/or angling being totally prohibited. In many parts of Scotland, for example, private ownership can extend well down towards estuary mouth, often including beaches that might look as though they are a part of the open foreshore. Once again it pays to check before you fish. In other areas, angling clubs have the sole right to fishing access.

Over the years many anglers have been caught and fined for catching and taking sea trout and salmon without permission. Salmon and sea trout are not eligible in most competitions but both of these species can be fairly common 'by-catches' when spinning or float fishing in certain estuaries. Before they can be legally taken you will, firstly, have to buy an NRA migratory trout and salmon rod licence and, secondly, confirm the game fishing rights are not privately owned. The illegal taking of game fish is a very serious crime, possibly resulting in a prison sentence.

1 Looking at estuaries

What is an estuary?

My dictionary describes an estuary as, 'the tidal mouth of a river' – an accurate description of an estuary in its most basic form. The countless estuaries around our coastline defy geographical stereotyping, however, although they do, essentially, remain the tidal mouths of various rivers, streams and tidal creeks that over many thousands of years have helped to create them.

The simplest type of estuary

The simplest and most basic type of estuary is found where a small stream or river tumbles directly into the sea. Here, typically, high mountain ranges run right up to the shoreline and the coastline often consists of very hard bed rock. In these estuaries the tidal differential may have little or no effect on the daily height of water behind the river mouth. The flooding tide might perhaps slow or slightly reverse the seaward flow of water from the river and may create one or two tidal 'sea pools' along the last few hundred yards of the rivers course, but the water within the estuary will be almost entirely fresh with little if any salt content. This will have considerable bearing on those species that will be found here, as will be seen later.

The lower reaches of the River Ogmore in South Wales. A small estuary often overlooked by anglers, but capable of producing fine bags of flounder, bass, eels and sea trout.

Larger estuaries

On lower coastal plains, where rivers gradually deepen and widen out on their journey towards the sea, the estuary often assumes its more usual form – that of a broad expanse of tidal water gently snaking its way towards the sea. Often the actual mouth of the estuary will be relatively small in relation to the size of the tidal plain and backwaters inland. In some cases huge natural harbours may be formed, Poole Harbour in Dorset being a very good example.

Usually there will be a distinct and twice daily tidal cycle, when the main current switches direction and flows inland, often with tremendous force. At low water vast expanses of the river basin will be left high and dry leaving complex systems of sandbanks exposed. Many of these banks will be dissected and drained by deep channels. These channels mark the main course of the river bed and form the routes along which many fish will make their way towards the upper reaches of the estuary

A typical mid-sized estuary. This is the Cloghane Estuary in Co Kerry, Ireland. Note the main channel, along which fish will generally move inshore with the flooding tide before they spread out and search for food over the sandbanks and amongst the weed and rocks.

during the flooding tide. One of the main features in this sort of estuary, and one that can affect the fishing and the types of fish present, is the massive variation in salt levels which occur on a daily basis. When the tide is at its ebb, the volume of fresh water flowing down through the estuary will constantly dilute the salt water, so that by low tide it may be pure fresh water only flowing into the sea. This is particularly so at times of heavy rainfall or when snow on distant mountains is thawing. Add to this the various pollutants running off the land, and you have a powerful deterrent to any inland migration of fish.

As the next tide starts to flood, salt water from the sea will steadily move inland. Often termed a saltwater wedge, it will gradually increase the salinity level and bring with it those species of fish with minimal tolerance of fresh or brackish conditions. The distance that this 'wedge' of salt water moves inland will depend on several factors, such as the strength of freshwater flow, the size of the tide and the local topography; all are factors for the estuary angler to consider.

Deltas and inland seas

At the largest end of the estuary scale there are the huge tidal deltas, such as the Thames Estuary and the Bristol Channel. Such is the vast expanse of these great waterways that many anglers consider them as the open sea. Often the nearest foreshore might be several miles away. In reality, however, they are enormous communal estuaries, displaying on a far grander scale all of the characteristics found in an estuary formed by a single river.

There will almost certainly be distinct tidal cycles and often the tide will run with tremendous force. At most times the salinity of the water will vary between brackish and pure salt water, and the variety of species the angler can expect to encounter will be large. Consequently there is scope for employing a great many angling methods and techniques. In essence, fishing within this type of estuary will be exactly the same as fishing in the open sea.

Lastly there are the fjords and sea lochs, not estuaries in the true sense of the word as defined by a dictionary, but similar in many ways. The geographical fact is that these are really inland seas. Some, such as Milford Haven in West Wales, will have several rivers running

Fishing the larger estuaries such as the Bristol Channel is often more akin to fishing the open sea. Here, an angler fishing the mudflats at Redwick in South Wales attempts to present a bait at long range. Sound terminal tackle is essential to prevent serious accidents.

into them. Although, in general, they contain a far greater depth and volume of water than a more typical estuary, many species of fish will take up residence and behave just as they would in a normal river estuary.

The attraction of estuaries

So, what is it that attracts sea fish to an estuary in the first place? After all, the water within most estuaries is rarely as clean as that found offshore. Large quantities of silt are present in suspension and, more often than not these days, significant levels of pollution.

Many species of fish can adapt to and tolerate varying levels of salt in water by a process called osmosis. Pure water can pass through animal membrane but the various different salts that are dissolved in water cannot. When two different solutions with different concentrations of salts are separated by such a membrane, water will pass from the weaker solution towards the stronger, thus diluting the strongest solution until both solutions are of equal strength.

In the sea this is a very gradual process which occurs through the fish's gills. Fish will inhabit areas of water where the salt content is to their liking, usually choosing to leave at times when the salinity level is falling – that is when the river is in flood following heavy rain. The salinity level is frequently far lower within the confines of an estuary than out at sea, yet many species of fish, including some of those most prized by anglers, will tolerate these brackish and dirty conditions.

The reason for this tolerance is very simple: food! A few species enter estuaries for shelter or in order to breed, but it is generally an abundance of food that is the biggest attraction. Most estuaries pay host to a vast wealth of marine life and maintain entire food chains, from the tiniest sand flea right through to large predatory fish. Within the sheltered confines of the estuary, well away from the near-constant pounding and scouring action of waves and swell on the more open beaches, such a rich variety of food thrives.

The mean water temperature within a typical estuary will often be several degrees higher than out at sea, and this also will help to provide a favourable habitat for all sorts of life. At low tide the sun very quickly warms the sands, tidal mudbeds and shallow rock pools, providing ideal growth and breeding conditions for the millions of insects, crustaceans and fish that live there. In addition, most inland brackish waters are rich in basic nutrients, a further factor that helps maintain the food chain.

Many types of marine worm can be found within estuaries, often forming sizeable colonies in the various sand and mudbanks. Substantial populations of common shore crabs are perfectly at home living in the mud and weed, with ample places in which to make a safe retreat when the tide ebbs away. In addition to the worms and crabs, most estuaries support sizeable colonies of shellfish such as cockles, mussels, clams and razorfish. Sandeels, blennies, gobies and the fry of many different species of fish are also common, as well as countless prawns and shrimps – food aplenty for larger fish.

Benefits of fishing estuaries

One of the major benefits for the angler who fishes the tidal estuary is that, by visiting the venue at low water, he or she

can study the actual topography of the area that will ultimately be fished. This will be invaluable, and should allow the angler to select areas where fish are likely to migrate and feed as the tide floods.

With the first push of the flooding tide many fish start their twice daily journey into the estuary. Initially they follow the deeper creeks and drainage channels, mentioned earlier, and when there is sufficient water depth they fan out across the flats. A comprehensive study of the area at low water, noting all features, certainly pays dividends when it's time to return with the rod. Fish visit weed beds, rock pools, sand and mudbanks in search of the rich pickings of food to be found there and these make excellent places for the angler to present baits.

One of the very best times to recce an estuary is at low water on a spring tide. A spring tide is one of the largest tides, occurring twice a month. During 'springs' the tide not only floods into the estuary further, giving a far greater height of water than normal, but ebbs back further, leaving vast expanses of the seabed exposed that normally remain covered.

Safety in estuaries

Often the optimum time to fish an estuary is when the tide is flooding but,

Once again this is the Cloghane Estuary in southern Ireland. In this shot note the deep drainage channel at the base of the weed and rocks. It looks as though it ought to hold fish, and it does. At high tide a lob of about 20 yards into this channel is all that is needed to catch fish.

in many areas, there is a danger of the flooding tide cutting off your retreat by back-filling gullies. By previously sitting back and observing how a tide floods across an area you will not only be able to anticipate the movements of fish, but you will also be able to make a mental note of those places that get cut off by the tide, and also the stages of the tide which are safe to fish.

Be particularly cautious when venturing out across mudflats and areas of salt marsh. These might well be safe enough to walk across at low tide, but even an inch of water covering mud can quickly conceal deep holes and drainage channels that were easy enough to see at low tide. This is particularly the case when fishing the larger estuaries, as a walk of several hundred yards or more might be necessary in order to reach the water line at low water. Over the years many anglers have drowned as a result of getting stuck in mud or cut off by the flooding tide.

14

Always exercise particular caution when fishing at night, and don't forget the ever-present danger of fog, a common feature of many estuaries during the autumn. A walk of a hundred yards back to safety across the mudflats can be a totally different proposition if fog suddenly arrives. It is a good idea to carry a compass whenever there is a particularly long walk to the water's edge and, obviously, a good reliable light at night.

Safety afloat

Afloat, too, many boat anglers wrongly assume that because they are fishing within close proximity of land they are safer than if they were fishing in the open sea. This is a big mistake! Sea conditions within an estuary can be as bad, and often far worse, than out in the open sea.

The strength of the tide is frequently far stronger within an estuary than in open water. The Bristol Channel experiences the second highest rise and fall of tide in the world, which equates to a 38ft tidal range at Barry during spring tides. The run of water is awesome and has to be experienced to be believed. Many small boats have got into difficulty simply because they have underestimated the strength of the tide. The tide will be at its worst when the wind is blowing against it, as this can very quickly create areas of rough and turbulent water.

Sandbanks and generally shallow conditions pose an ever-present risk of running aground for the careless navigator. A good depth sounder and a large-scale sea chart are essential. Be extra cautious near the mouth of the estuary, especially if there is a sand bar running across it. These are notorious for creating extremely rough seas, usually more so when the tide is at ebb with an opposing wind.

Many estuaries are home to commercial shipping ports. Most of the ships that visit these ports are constrained by their draft, and therefore can only navigate within the main channels. There have been many instances of small craft impeding the passage of shipping within estuaries. Not only is this dangerous, but in most cases the smaller boats are contravening international maritime law, and face the real possibility of hefty fines if they are caught. It is essential that you are fully aware of all features found within an estuary before you put to sea.

Locals fishing for flounder on the Teign in South Devon. Anyone who does not know the local ground well would be foolhardy to risk staying in such a position.

2 Tackle for estuary fishing

The tackle the sea angler uses should mostly be chosen to suit the prevailing conditions and the technique the angler intends using; the target species of fish is often far less important. Freshwater anglers frequently land double-figure fish on incredibly light breaking strains of line, but they do not have the rigours of the tides, waves, and snag-ridden sea bed to contend with when presenting baits and playing fish in the sea.

For example, consider an angler who intends to fish a mark at long range for whiting – fish with an average size of less than 1lb in weight. The fact that the baits must be cast a fair way will probably demand a stiff beachcaster matched with a multiplier reel loaded with 15lb BS – an outfit capable of hurling 5oz of lead, plus baits, 100 yards or more out to sea. Of course, such an outfit will be over-gunning the sporting potential of even the biggest whiting that the angler is ever likely to hook, but it is needed, firstly, to present the bait at the required distance and, secondly, to hold firm on the sea bed and counteract the strong pull of the tide.

Conversely, an angler freelining a whole peeler crab or mackerel head for bass along the margins of a tidal creek will be more than adequately equipped with a light spinning rod and a small fixed spool reel loaded with 8lb line or even less. His target species often reaches 5lb, and far bigger specimens are always

possible, yet the fishing conditions allow the use of light and sporting tackle as the bait can easily be lobbed the required distance. With minimal run of tide, the presentation of that bait will actually be enhanced by allowing it to roll gently to and fro with the current.

The following list of outfits are only intended as a guide, and quite often specific situations will require a more specialist approach. The angler should always feel free, and indeed encouraged, to experiment with different types of tackle other than that normally used at a particular venue. But, more often than not, the tackle listed below will prove adequate under most situations.

There has never been a larger range of fishing tackle in the shops. The novice can be forgiven for becoming totally bewildered when faced with rack upon rack of rods, and cabinets full of reels. Don't be conned into buying the most expensive gear available in the false belief that you will fish better with it. In all probability you will not. In the case of high performance beach rods and reels you will probably fare far worse with a top of the range outfit than with a more reasonably priced and manageable one.

It must be mentioned here, and I make no apologies for further remarks throughout this book, that it is primarily the bait that catches the fish. The latest and greatest rods, reels and accessories can sometimes help, but presenting the right bait, in the right place and at the right time should be every angler's goal. Only then will the angler be in with a chance of regular success.

Shore-fishing tackle

Standard beachcasting outfit

This is usually a 12ft or 13ft beach-caster, capable of casting leads of 5–6oz. This outfit will be required for fishing at long range in the larger estuaries, or anywhere where distance is required, or where there is a strong run of tide. The rod should be matched with either a fixed spool or multiplier reel, loaded with nylon monofilament line between 12lb and 18lb BS. A shockleader should also be used; this is a short length of strong line, usually with a minimum breaking strain of 50lb, used to absorb the power of the cast and thus prevent dangerous crack-offs.

Buying a beachcasting rod that is far too powerful for their casting style is a mistake many anglers make. Powerful rods do not automatically cast big distances. It will ultimately be your casting style that determines how well the rod performs. Powerful rods are extremely stiff and require a sound and powerful casting style in order to bend them and make them work. This cannot be achieved with the standard overhead thump, and a more forgiving blank will ultimately prove to be of greater use until one develops the necessary skill to enable one to use a stronger rod.

Light beachcaster/bass rod

The next outfit will be a light beach-caster or a purpose-made bass rod,

about 11ft in length. The rod should be capable of comfortably casting leads of between 2oz and 4oz reasonable distances, allowing for the addition of bait. Either a small multiplier or a fixed spool, which will probably be loaded with line between 10lb and 15lb BS, is ideal for use with this rod. This is an excellent 'all-round estuary outfit', with a wide range of useful applications.

Spinning/float rod

The lightest outfit needed by the shore angler will be a light rod suitable for spinning and float fishing, in addition to freelining baits or legering with light

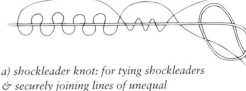

a) shockleader knot: for tying shockleaders & securely joining lines of unequal thickness

b) Uni-knot: excellent all-round knot for tying on hooks, swivels, etc.

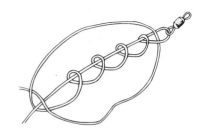

c) Tucked half blood knot: another strong all-round knot

Fig. 1 Selection of useful knots.

leads of up to 2oz. Either an off-the-shelf spinning rod of between 8ft and 10ft or a slightly longer specialist carp or pike rod will be ideal. The best reel to complete the outfit will be a small fixed spool, loaded with either 8lb or 10lb BS line. Many light outfits tend to be far too 'sloppy', and it is advisable to look for an outfit with plenty of inherent strength built into it. This does not necessarily mean buying a poker-stiff rod.

Boat-fishing tackle

Uptide outfit

Uptiding, or boatcasting as it is also known, originated in the Thames Estuary, and wherever boat fishing is practised in estuaries uptiding is invariably the most popular method. Uptide rods are rated in casting weights, giving an indication of the size of lead that the rod is capable of casting. A good all-round uptider should be able comfortably to handle leads of 4–6oz, but lighter or heavier rods may well be more suited in some areas, or for specialist applications – fishing light for flatfish and whiting for example. Most anglers use multiplier reels for uptiding. However, it is possible to use a decent-quality fixed spool.

When buying an uptider, there are three important features you should look for. In addition to quality rings and a reel seat, the rod should have a sensitive tip for bite detection. Secondly, the middle third of the rod should be gutsy enough to handle decent fish in a strong run of tide, yet not so stiff that casting will be difficult. There should be sufficient 'give' in the tip and middle to prevent grip leads from being prematurely broken out as the boat rocks at anchor, or when fishing in rough conditions. The butt section or lower third of the blank should be

sufficiently stiff to provide the power to handle big fish in strong tides.

Light boat rod

Unlike uptiders, traditional downtide boat rods are rated in line classes, which give an approximate indication of the breaking strain of line that is suitable to use with them. For example, a 12lb class rod is ideal to use with lines between 10lb BS and 15lb BS, and lines between 15lb BS and about 25lb BS are ideal for use with a 20lb class rod.

Both of these rods are ideal for light estuary work, but perhaps a 30lb class rod may be needed when fishing deep water with a strong run of tide. When downtiding, a multiplier reel really is the best tool to use, but a fixed spool reel can be useful when fishing on the drift using a light 6lb or 12lb class rod. Look for a rod with a fine tip for maximum sensitivity, in addition to quality fixtures and fittings.

Spinning outfit

A light spinning rod also has its place in boat fishing, not only for casting various types of lures, but for bait fishing as well. It is generally preferable to choose a slightly shorter spinning rod for fishing afloat than perhaps you would use from the shore; not only is a long rod a bit of a nuisance and cumbersome in a small boat, but many anglers find that big fish are far easier to handle with a shorter rod. Either a fixed spool or multiplier reel will be ideal to match with this rod.

Terminal tackle

Most anglers tend to carry far too much terminal tackle. Really, all they actually need in most situations is a selection of different sizes of hooks in one or two patterns, a few swivels and links and a few weights. Paternoster booms, bait clips, beads and other bits and bobs can help to improve bait presentation in many situations, but they are not always essential.

I feel that there is a growing tendency to over-complicate fishing, and terminal rigs in particular. Rigs are nearly always most effective when kept as simple as possible. If some anglers put half as much effort into their bait presentation as they do into creating complex terminal rigs, then they would almost certainly catch more fish.

The answer is initially to buy a minimal selection of 'quality' items of terminal tackle. It might be tempting to save a few pence on cheap items of doubtful origin, but the error in this will soon be seen the first time a decent fish straightens a hook or snaps a swivel. I do not intend patronizing any tackle manufacturers in this book, but I do feel it is necessary to recommend the products of certain companies in this section, in order to guide the novice in the right direction.

Various rig diagrams are used through-out the book to illustrate suitable and popular end rigs. However, the actual dimensions and format given for each rig are flexible, and any of the rigs can, and should, be adapted to suit certain conditions. For example, the methods given for attaching a rotten bottom can be used on all sorts of different rigs. The lengths of the hook snoods on the various rigs are totally flexible, and can be either shortened or lengthened as conditions dictate.

Never be afraid to experiment in any form of angling. The difference between total failure and a resounding success might just be an extra few inches added

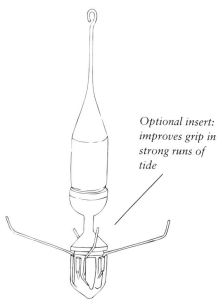

Optional insert: improves grip in strong runs of tide

Grip wires trip out individually and need not be attached until required, making transporting and storing the leads a lot easier

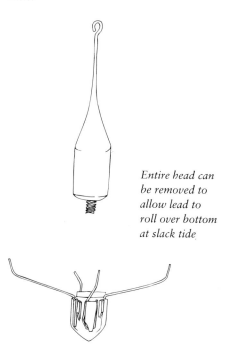

Entire head can be removed to allow lead to roll over bottom at slack tide.

Fig. 2 Gemini breakout-type leads.

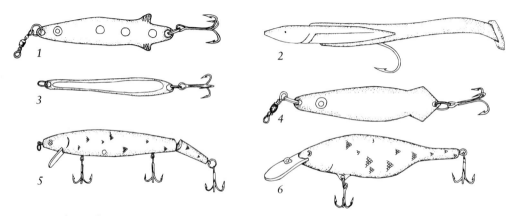

1 & 4 Toby-type spoons for general spinning   3 Long thin lure for extra distance
2 Artificial sandeel   5 & 6 Floating plugs

Fig. 3   Selection of artificial lures.

or removed from a hooklength, or swapping a grip lead for a plain bomb and allowing the tide to gently roll a bait across the bottom.

When it comes to choosing hooks, Mustad produce a range covering every situation that the sea angler is likely to encounter. Initially just two patterns in a range of sizes will suffice. For general boat fishing and shore fishing, Mustads bronzed Viking range (Ref 79515BR) adequately cover all situations. For more delicate presentation of smaller baits, when fishing for smaller fish, or when livebaiting with prawns or sandeels, Mustads Aberdeen hooks (Ref 3261BLN) are superb. Both of these ranges have recently been upgraded and now feature a super sharp point straight out of the box.

For swivels and links, I would also not hesitate to recommend Mustad, but companies like Berkley and Samco also produce swivels of excellent quality. Mustad's split ovals are probably the strongest and safest links available on the market today for attaching lead weights to traces.

Many companies produce quality line. But it should be remembered that any line is only as strong as its weakest section. Many hi-tech lines are not only very expensive, but, being made with minimal diameter, they are often very prone to damage when fishing over rough ground. My own policy is to avoid paying for expensive line, preferring to buy more economical brands, which I can afford to change on a regular basis. My own favourites are Maxima and Sylcast, both of which are very affordable, knot well, have a good resistance to abrasion, and over many years have proved to be very reliable. I use both for main lines and shock leaders, in suitable breaking strains. Maxima is a particularly good line for spinning.

Never consider buying lead weights from a tackle shop, unless you are very rich! Moulds covering all popular shapes and sizes are readily available, and lead is easily begged, borrowed or swapped. Making breakout type grip leads, which are particularly expensive in shops, used to be a problem, but not any more. The arrival of the Gemini system a few years ago has revolutionized sinker technology, and parts and individual components are now readily available to make your own high quality break out leads.

The biggest advantage with the Gemini leads are that the grip wires need not be attached until needed, making stowage and transport a lot easier and safer. The tension at which the wires trip can be quickly increased, or decreased, as conditions dictate. Lastly, unlike traditional breakout leads, the wires on the Gemini trip individually, so, in the event of a lead prematurely tripping, there are still three other wires which should regrip, and prevent the lead dragging into a snag (Fig. 2).

Lures (Fig. 3)

A minimal selection of spinners and spoons will cover most situations. Toby type spoons and the tried and trusted German Sprat are both excellent all-rounders. For the past few years I have used the Bridun Lance for long-range, deep water work, and the Kilty Kerryman for more general applications. Both are excellent lures and come highly recommended. Carry a range between ½oz and 1oz.

The next most useful artificial is the rubber sandeel, which is perfect for both spinning and trolling from a boat. Again a few different sizes, in a range of colours, will generally suffice. Predatory fish such as bass frequently become pre-occupied by feeding on sandeels, and at these times an artificial sandeel can be a deadly lure.

Recent years have seen a resurgence of interest in the use of artificial plugs, mainly for bass. Hundreds of different types are now widely available, but half a dozen jointed Rapalas or Rebels in different colours should be all you need. The most useful sizes are between 3½in and 5in. Floating plugs are particularly useful when fishing shallow water or rough ground marks.

The baited spoon is the classic estuary lure from both boat and shore, and these can either be bought, or they can be very easily made from old household spoons. Lastly, a few strings of mackerel feathers or their modern alternatives should be kept in every angler's tackle box (Fig. 4).

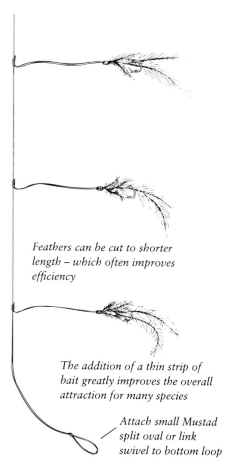

Attach a small swivel to top hook

Feathers can be cut to shorter length – which often improves efficiency

The addition of a thin strip of bait greatly improves the overall attraction for many species

Attach small Mustad split oval or link swivel to bottom loop

* *Note: few sets of shop-bought feathers are tied from line strong enough to withstand the power of even a moderate cast. Always exercise extreme caution when casting feathers*

Fig. 4 Traditional mackerel feathers.

21

3 Baits

An estuary provides fish with a well-stocked larder of food, and the angler with a plentiful supply of bait. To buy bait from the tackle shop is expensive, and rarely is shop-bought bait as effective as bait which has been dug or collected fresh. Indeed, locally obtained bait will often outfish bait collected from another venue when the two are used side by side. There is also a certain amount of satisfaction in arriving at an estuary just before low water, and spending an hour or so rummaging around in the rock pools or digging the sand and mudbank for fresh bait. Then, when the new tide starts creeping inland, using this bait to catch a fish or two.

Crab

An increasing number of anglers have started using crab for more of their fishing, and as a result are catching a lot more fish. Crab really is an excellent all-round bait, few fish will bypass a fresh lump of prime peeler crab oozing juices out into the tide.

The sort of crabs that make excellent bait are known as peelers or soft-back crabs. Hard-back crabs, although frequently found inside the stomachs of fish, are rarely a successful hookbait, except for specialist applications such as when fishing for wrasse or smooth hounds.

The hard outer shell of the crab is known as the exo-skeleton, and it both supports and protects the delicate body mass and internal organs. In order to grow, the crab must first develop a new shell within its existing one. At this stage the new shell is extremely soft and is partly developed by the crab extracting calcium from its old shell. During this process, the old, outer shell becomes very brittle, and it is at this stage that the crab is known as a peeler.

When it is ready to moult its outer shell, the crab crawls under a stone or hides in some other inaccessible and safe spot, hopefully out of reach of hungry predators. Next it draws in water in order to swell its inner body, splitting the outer shell in the process. The crab is now in peak condition to be used as bait. Finally, and with tremendous effort, the crab crawls and pushes itself free of its old shell, and is left as a soft blob of jelly in its bright new livery. At this stage it is known as a soft crab, and is also an excellent bait. Over the next few days the new skin will gradually crispen and harden off until, after about a week, the shell will be fully hardened and the crab will be fairly safe from predators again.

In most areas crabs peel twice a year, once in the spring, and again in late summer or early autumn, although there are normally a few to be found in peeling condition throughout the summer. In the south-west crabs peel throughout the year, and it is usually only during prolonged cold periods that none are available.

The best places to look for peeler crabs are in shallow rock pools, beneath stones, buried in the mud and sand at the bottom of groynes or harbour walls, under thick beds of seaweed, inside old tyres and tin cans – anywhere, in fact, where the crab can crawl into relative safety.

In many estuaries you will come across neatly regimented lines of roof slates or old pieces of pipe and guttering stuck in the sand and mud. These look like ideal hidey-holes for crabs, and indeed they are, but they have been put there by anglers and commercial bait dealers for just this reason. Leave them alone. Not only will you be interfering with someone else's livelihood or bait supply, but you could end up with a thick ear or worse, as crab traps are very closely guarded.

Below Searching for peeler crabs, among the rocks and weed at low tide.

The easiest way to identify a peeler crab from a hard back is by very gently twisting the last segment of one of its legs. If the crab is in the peeling stage the joint will come away easily, leaving a new and perfectly formed leg beneath. If the crab is not a peeler then there will be a white sinewy strand, and the crab should be returned. Also, the rear of the crab's shell starts to split and then lift as the crab prepares to peel. Always carefully return any stones that you have lifted, not only for the benefit of crabs, but for all of the marine life in the area.

Above A common shore peeler crab, in the peak of condition for use as bait.

Provided they are kept cool and moist, peeler crabs can be kept in prime condition for many weeks. The ideal way to store them is to keep them in a domestic fridge, set at about 5°C (or a medium setting). Keep them in moist seaweed, and give them a daily drink of clean sea water.

The commonest crabs are the green shore crabs. In the lower reaches of some estuaries you may also come across the edible and velvet swimming crab in peeling condition. These make outstanding baits, but they tend to be far more difficult to store in the long term, requiring saltwater aquariums with filters and airpumps. Both species dislike fresh or brackish water and you are more likely to find them as you get closer to the open sea. Look near the extreme low water mark on the biggest tides, usually in the deeper rock pools.

Blow lugworm

Of the two species of lugworm the blow lug are by far the commonest and colonies are often found well within the estuary, although the larger worms often live nearest the sea. Blow lug are found in both mud and sand banks. Their location is clearly given away by the familiar casts and blow holes on the surface, which start to show a few hours after the ebb tide has receded (Fig. 5).

Digging enough worms for a fishing session is relatively easy, but it does require a certain knack in order to make light work of it. In soft mud a narrow spade will be the best tool for the job, whereas a potato fork with four flat tines is more suited to digging drier areas of mud and sand. Where the casts are thickest on the ground simply digging a trench through the area of highest concentration will uncover the worms, which are usually about 1½–2 spits deep.

Where the casts are thinner on the ground the worms will have to be dug out individually. The easiest method is to draw an imaginary line between the cast and the blow hole, and place your fork or spade midway between them, at an angle of 90° to this line. First remove sand to a depth of half a spit, then move the fork back to a position just behind the cast. The worm will be lying in a U-shaped burrow head towards the blow hole, and by carefully removing a full spit from this position the worm should be uncovered intact. In very cold weather or when there is a lot of rainwater lying on the surface, the casts and holes might be difficult to locate, and the worms a lot deeper in the sand.

Blow lug from different areas keep with varying degrees of success, but in general most blow lug will be at their best if used within a day or so of digging. Keep your worms cool and moist, either in seaweed or clean sand. Some blow lug keep best if laid out flat in trays of clean sea water and stored in a fridge. Never

Fig. 5   Diagram of blow lug burrow.

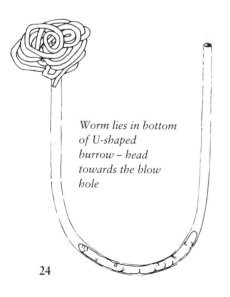

Worm lies in bottom of U-shaped burrow – head towards the blow hole

Estuaries supply the angler with a bountiful supply of different baits. Here anglers dig for blow lug in southern Ireland. There digging acts as groundbait for foraging fish when the tide comes in.

Right Prime blow lug, top-quality bait for a multitude of different species.

mix broken or sick-looking worms with those that are fresh and healthy, as they will very quickly infect and destroy your entire stock.

Black lugworms

Black lugs are the biggest of the lugworms, and make an exceptional bait for many species, notably cod. They are found in near-vertical burrows on or very near, the extreme low water mark. They have little, if any, tolerance of fresh water, so the area around the mouth of the estuary will often be the best place to look.

The cast thrown out by a black lug is a lot smaller and neater than the blow lug, and often forms a perfect 'Catherine wheel' on the surface, about the size of a two pence piece. There is a very small blow hole very close to the cast, rarely visible until you disturb the burrow. Black lug are either dug with a spade by following the hole beneath the cast down to the worm, or they can be pumped using a bait pump. Both techniques require a lot of skill, so don't expect too many worms on your first digging session or two.

25

Black lug keep in prime condition for up to a week and often longer. The best way to keep them is by first gutting the worms, by gently squeezing the guts out through the head, and then storing them in shallow trays of clean sea water in a refrigerator. Alternatively, they can be individually rolled in newspaper, but this has a tendency to dry the worm out. Black lug both freeze and salt very well. To freeze the worms simply gut them and lie them on kitchen paper for about half an hour. Then roll them individually in newspaper and place in the freezer in conveniently sized packs. To salt the worms, dry them out as before, then give them a liberal and complete coating of salt. Salted worms keep for many weeks when stored in the fridge or freezer.

King ragworms

King rags are the largest and most common of the ragworms, and the most widely used by anglers. They are generally found in a mixture of sand and mud, usually where there is a fair amount of shale or shell grit in the area. They are reasonably tolerant of brackish conditions, but may favour those areas with a higher salt level. Occasionally the location of their burrows is given away by small blow holes, but unlike the lugworm they do not throw out a tell-tail cast.

The nature of the ground where ragworms are found usually dictates that a fork with narrow tines is the best implement for digging them out. Digging a quantity of ragworms usually entails a lot of hard work.

Of all of the species of marine worms the king rag is by far the easiest to keep and store in the long term. The usual method is to wrap them in newspaper with a few handfuls of peat to absorb any juice secreted by the worms. Never be tempted to store too many worms in one packet, ragworms have a fierce set of pincers mounted on their heads which they will use to damage any other worms lying in close contact.

Some anglers tank their ragworms in marine aquaria. Kept in such a way, the worms keep in top physical condition for many weeks, but there are doubts about the fish-catching qualities of tanked rag. Some anglers believe many of the vital body juices and scents are lost over a period of time.

White ragworms

White rags are one of the hardest species of ragworm to locate in large quantities. They are highly prized by match anglers, who have great faith in the worms' qualities as a visual attractor, often fishing them as part of a cocktail bait. They have little tolerance of fresh water, and are rarely found far from the open sea. Typically, white rag live in clean coral sand, often a few are turned up when digging lugworms.

White rag must be kept in very clean sea water. The water must be changed two or three times a day, especially during the first two days of storage. It is imperative that any sick-looking worms are removed instantly, as they will very quickly contaminate and kill off the rest of the stock.

Harbour ragworms

Commonly known as maddies, harbour ragworms are readily available in most estuaries, and are fairly tolerant of brackish water. Harbour rag are frequently found towards the tidal limit of the estuary.

They live in the thick, grey mud, so

often typical of the inter-tidal zone in many estuaries, and collecting them can be a very messy business indeed! When the mud is of a fairly heavy consistency, they can be dug with either a fork or spade, while in softer mud the easiest way to uncover the worms is by hand. Always exercise extreme caution when grubbing about in the mud for harbour rag, or any other type of bait, as most estuaries are unfortunately full of broken glass and rusting cans, especially around harbours.

These worms are best collected fresh on the day they are going to be used, as they do not keep as well as the larger species of worms. Measuring up to about 2in, harbour rag are a very soft and delicate bait requiring careful handling. They are usually fished in bunches on fine wired hooks for flatties and eels. They also make a deadly bait for mullet, flounder, bass and sea trout, especially when mounted on the hooks of a small bar-spoon-type spinner.

Fish (Fig. 6)

Various types of fish are used as bait by sea anglers. Mackerel is by far the most readily available and therefore widely used, but in some areas herring, which make excellent cut bait, can be caught. In addition, more and more anglers are beginning to appreciate the benefits of using a small pouting, poor cod, whiting, rockling or other species for livebait. Most of the biggest bass and cod caught each year fall to fish bait, and an increasingly high proportion of these to livebaits.

The normal way to catch mackerel and herring is by using a traditional set of feathers, or their modern alternatives such as Hokeye lures which are far more effective (Fig. 7). Mackerel shoal in

a

a) This method allows the fish a greater freedom of movement, increasing its efficient life span, and increasing its attraction in the water. The fish is attached to the hook using a short loop of fishing line as shown

b) Many anglers attach livebait by lip-hooking.

b

Fig. 6　Two methods of attaching a livebait to a hook.

the lower reaches of many estuaries, especially towards high tide throughout the summer and autumn. Herring are not so widely available, but there are signs that the species is making a strong come-back. These days they can often be caught throughout the winter and autumn in many of the western sea lochs. Other species of fish are best caught on tiny pieces of worm or strips of fish on tiny hooks.

Fresh fish caught on the day is nearly always a far superior bait than shop-bought or frozen fish. The golden rule when using fish, as with most baits, is to match the size of your bait to the species of fish that you are targeting. For

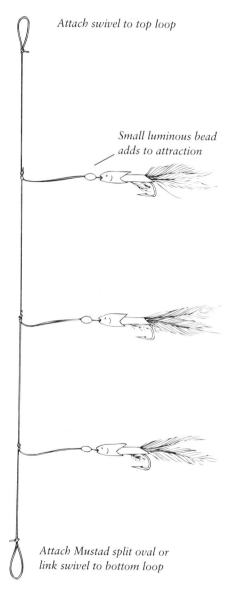

Attach swivel to top loop

Small luminous bead adds to attraction

Attach Mustad split oval or link swivel to bottom loop

Fig. 7 Mustad Hokeye tempter rig.

example, when fishing for whiting thin bite-sized strips no more than an inch long are ideal, but if you are targeting specimen bass a head and guts will make a far more appropriate and more tempting offering.

Sandeels

Sandeels, which are an important component of the marine food chain, form the major part of the diet of most predatory fish and therefore make an excellent bait. The ideal way to fish sandeels is as a livebait, but the dead eels, fresh or frozen and either fished whole or in chunks, are also excellent.

Live sandeels are readily available in the south-west, either from tackle shops, whose owners are increasingly installing tanks so that they can stock them on the premises, or from commercial sandeel netters, based on several of the larger south coast estuaries such as the Teign and the Exe. More tackle shops well away from the south are also supplying live eels, as a greater awareness of their effectiveness as livebait increases demand. The greater sandeel or launce is often caught when feathering for mackerel.

You can also collect live eels by hand near the mouths of many estuaries. Towards low water the eels bury themselves in banks of clean coral sand and gravel near the extreme low water mark, especially in the vicinity of freshwater streams running across the sands. Occasionally they can be dug out, but the best method is to use a special tool known as a vingler.

A vingler is made by grinding the edge off a long bread knife, and filing the end into the shape of a blunt hook. This is then drawn through the sand to rake out the eels. Almost a sport in its own right, using a vingler efficiently requires a high amount of skill, but it is always a skill that is very well worth any angler acquiring.

In the short term live eels can be stored in a box, covered in either wet seaweed or a moist towel. They must be

Searching for sandeels at low tide using a vingler.

kept cool, so frozen cool packs are very useful. For longer-term storage, the best method is to keep them in a bucket of clean sea water, fitted with an aerator to keep the water oxygenated or to use a purpose-made livebait container which hangs in the water (Fig. 8). Sandeels can be kept very easily in aquaria, and I know several anglers who have kept them for months at a time.

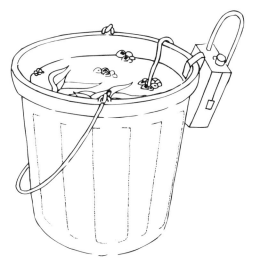

a) Bucket of seawater with portable battery-operated air pump

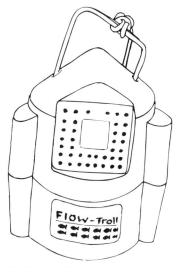

b) The flow troll bait container, the modern equivalent of the traditional courge. The flow troll is suspended in the sea – keeping baits in pristine condition. Access to the flow troll is via a hinged flap

Fig. 8   Methods of keeping livebaits alive.

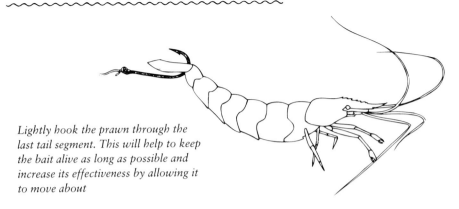

Lightly hook the prawn through the last tail segment. This will help to keep the bait alive as long as possible and increase its effectiveness by allowing it to move about

Prawns and shrimps

Prawns and shrimps are both under-used and are excellent baits, especially in and around tidal estuaries. Both can be netted out of rock pools along the low tide line, or around the base of harbour walls at low tide. Prawns can also be caught in a drop net, baited with an old fish head or other offal and suspended over the side of a pier, breakwater or dock wall.

Keep prawns and shrimps alive in a bucket of clean sea water, well aerated with an air pump. Both are best fished alive, typically on light float tackle. Live prawns can be freelined in the current on very light tackle, a very effective and sporting method for catching many species of fish (Fig. 9). Dead prawns are of limited use.

Razorfish (Fig. 10)

Razorfish are readily available at the mouth of many tidal estuaries, where they live in deep vertical burrows in clean sand. They are always found near the extreme low water mark on spring tides. The location of the burrow is given away by the 'keyhole'-shaped entrance on the surface, or by the occasional spouts of water that the razor fish ejects. They can either be dug or speared, using a specially fabricated spear with a barbed end, or simply salted. To salt razorfish simply

Fig. 9 Method of attaching a live prawn to a hook.

pour a thimbleful of ordinary dry table salt into the burrow, or alternatively squirt a highly concentrated saline solution down the hole using an old washing up liquid bottle. In a few minutes the razorfish will completely evacuate its burrow.

Razorfish can be kept live for up to a week by keeping them cool and giving them a daily drink of clean sea water. They freeze fairly well in their shells, though they tend to be very soft when they thaw out. Razorfish are a good all-round bait, and many anglers successfully fish razorfish in order to make part of a cocktail.

Mussels (Fig. 10)

Mussels are common in all estuaries, but only the larger ones are really of use for bait. Often found clinging to the rocks, weed, old pontoon supports or concrete groynes just below the high tide mark, mussels are, surprisingly, an under-used bait in many areas. The actual shellfish is extremely soft and delicate, and must be extricated carefully from its shell with a blunt knife if you are to keep it intact. It must then be gently bound on to the hook using fine elastic. It is a good all-round bait, particularly for cod and

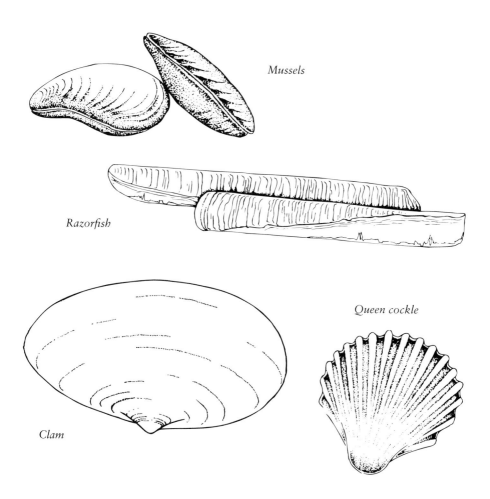

Mussels

Razorfish

Queen cockle

Clam

Fig. 10 A selection of shellfish baits.

flatfish. Mussels last for several days if kept cool and moist in a fridge.

Cockles

Cockles are one of our smallest shellfish, and are often uncovered when digging for other baits. They are excellent for flatfish and mullet and keep well for two or three days in the fridge. There are two species of cockle, the smaller common cockles, and the larger queen cockles which make a far superior bait.

Clams (Fig. 10)

Clams are often found in estuaries. One of our largest species of shellfish, clams live in deep burrows in sand and mud, indicated by a large hole on the surface. Unlike razorfish, clams are unable to move freely towards the surface and must be dug out with a spade or fork. A very useful bait either fished whole for bass or cod, or cut into smaller pieces for flatfish etc. They are best found following an onshore gale which often rips clams, as well as other shellfish, out of their burrows. They keep reasonably well in the fridge or an aerated bucket of cool sea water.

Squid (Fig. 11)

A very good all-round bait, squid can be caught on occasions, using either feathers or special multi-barb jigs. Boxes of frozen Californian squid can be bought very cheaply and can be used whole for bass, cod, and rays, or cut into long, thin strips for smaller species.

Earthworms

Earthworms can be a reasonable bait for catching flounders, eels and occasionally mullet in the upper reaches of the estuary, particularly after a flood. If used in the more saline lower reaches, however, earthworms very quickly bleach white and are then of little, if any, use.

Other baits

Sea anglers are constantly experimenting with different baits, and on their day most will catch a fish or two. Some species, notably mullet and bass can be caught on a wide and varied assortment of odd baits, such as bacon rind and sausage segments. Others baits such as bread paste, cheese and maggots can be quite effective, especially when used in conjunction with groundbait. Resident populations of fish can often be educated into eating certain foods. Often the reason why any particular population sticks around in one area is because there is an abundance of a certain type of food. The angler's prime objective should always be to try and discover what these fish are feeding on, and then use whatever it is on their hooks.

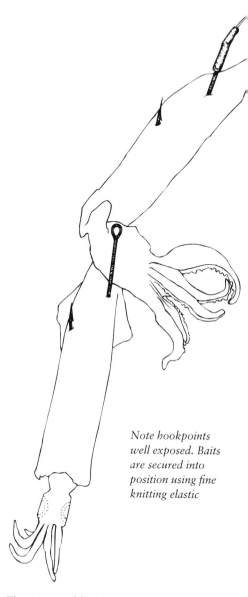

Note hookpoints well exposed. Baits are secured into position using fine knitting elastic

Fig. 11 Double calamari squid bait mounted on a pennel rig.

4 Shore-fishing techniques

Selecting a mark

When faced with the broad expanse of an estuary at low water, selecting an area to fish, and a suitable technique to use, can be very confusing. The ability to 'read the ground' will come with experience but there are certain features and habitats that are always worth exploring wherever they are found. But be warned; fish do not read angling books and simply because a particular gully or patch of weeds looks as if it ought to be attractive to fish it does not always follow that it is. Quite often featureless expanses of mud and sand can be very productive, and the lesson here is never to take anything for granted and always be prepared to experiment until you locate the fish.

Most features will be attractive to certain species of fish. For example, freshwater streams running into the main river channel will be likely spots for flounders and eels, and occasionally bass. Patches of weed and rock will have a broader appeal, possibly attracting bass, smooth hounds, pollack and cod, depending on geographical location and the time of year.

Deeper channels may attract tope, cod, dogfish and rays. Sandbanks and sand or gravel bars at the mouth of an estuary are excellent places to fish, using live sandeels, for bass, plaice and dabs. Wherever there are boat moorings, or around marinas and harbours, expect to find mullet cruising around the surface and bass lurking in wait for an easy meal in the shade provided by the boats. Over the years the tide will have scoured out depressions in the seabed near the support pilings of piers, breakwaters and harbour walls. These are excellent holding spots for flatfish and bass.

More or less any feature will be attractive to one or more species of fish, and the real skill is in first identifying the feature, next in anticipating which species of fish will be present, then, in deciding upon a suitable technique and bait and, finally, catching the fish.

Whenever fishing over clean and open ground it can sometimes be a good idea to keep your bait on the move, either by a slow gentle retrieve, or by using leads light enough to allow the tide and currents to gently roll the bait across the seabed. The exception, of course, is when you are fishing rough ground. Here it is essential to keep the rig firmly nailed to the seabed, to prevent it rolling into snags.

Long-range work

The ability to cast baits a long way is not always essential when fishing from the shore, indeed it can often be detrimental to success. However, there are many venues where it is necessary to be able to present baits at range.

When considering rigs suitable for fishing at long range, it is important to consider carefully the particular features of the venue, the type of bait you intend using, and the target species that you are after. The time to consider fishing at range is when you know or suspect fish will be attracted to, or passing by, a particular feature. Typically this might be a channel or rock ledge along which fish will travel in the tide, or perhaps a mussel bed or weedbed which they might visit in search of food.

When preparing baits for long range work a lot of consideration should be given to ensuring the bait is as neat, compact and streamlined as possible. If it is not, basic aerodynamics will prevent it from reaching the desired spot. To prepare a bait correctly so that it is not ripped apart by the initial force of a powerful cast, it is necessary to lash the bait securely on to the hook using fine knitting elastic, and then clip it on to the backbone of the trace to prevent it from flapping about.

Fishing at range over clean ground is relatively straightforward, provided your casting is up to scratch, and you follow the basic guidelines laid out above. When fishing a decent sized bait, perhaps for cod, rays or smooth hounds, a single paternoster hook rig will usually be ideal. When targeting smaller species, perhaps flounder, dabs or whiting, then a two or even three-hook, clipped paternoster rig will be preferable (Fig. 12).

Occasionally, when after smaller fish you may get a larger fish picking up your bait. In this instance the wishbone rig offers the best of both worlds. With two small baits lying side by side there will be the attraction of a single large bait, with double the hooking potential of a single small hook (Fig. 13).

A peeler crab bait ready for use and mounted on to a pennel rig – a superb bait for many species. Note that fine knitting elastic has been used to ensure that the hook points remain exposed.

Long-range fishing over rough ground is a totally different ball game. The ever-present risk of getting snagged dictates several fundamental yet very important changes in the end rig. It will be necessary to incorporate a rotten bottom into the rig so that in the event of the lead snagging only the lead will be lost, not the rest of your terminal tackle – and possibly a good fish as well.

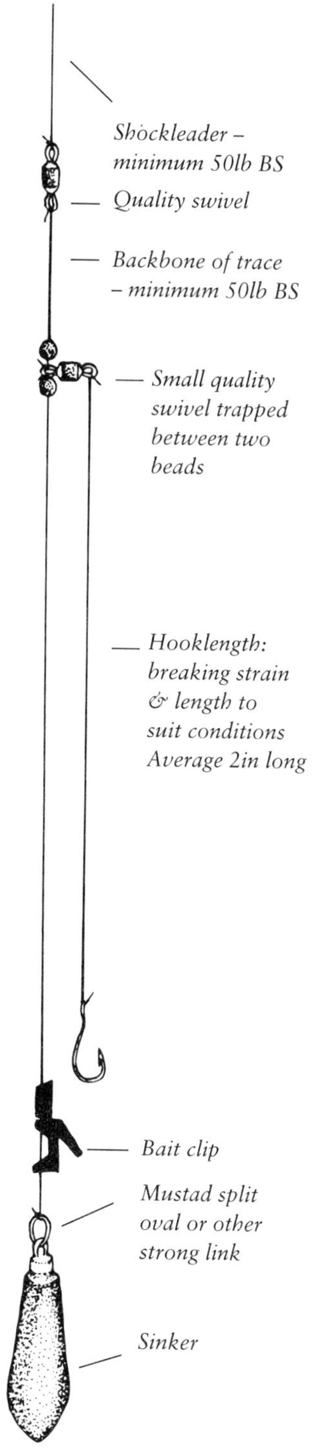

Shockleader –
minimum 50lb BS

Quality swivel

Backbone of trace
– minimum 50lb BS

Small quality
swivel trapped
between two
beads

Small quality swivel

Two equal length hooklengths

Hooklength:
breaking strain
& length to
suit conditions
Average 2in long

The advantages of this rig are
that the angler can fish 2
small baits on 2 small hooks,
allowing him to catch small
fish. However, the combined
size of the twin baits increases
the overall attraction of the
bait sufficiently to draw larger
fish, which then take either
one or both baits. Two hooks
increase the chances of
securing a firm hookhold in
sizeable fish

Bait clip

Mustad split
oval or other
strong link

Sinker

Twin baited hooks fish
alongside each other

Fig. 12   Fixed-clipped paternoster rig
for long-range fishing.

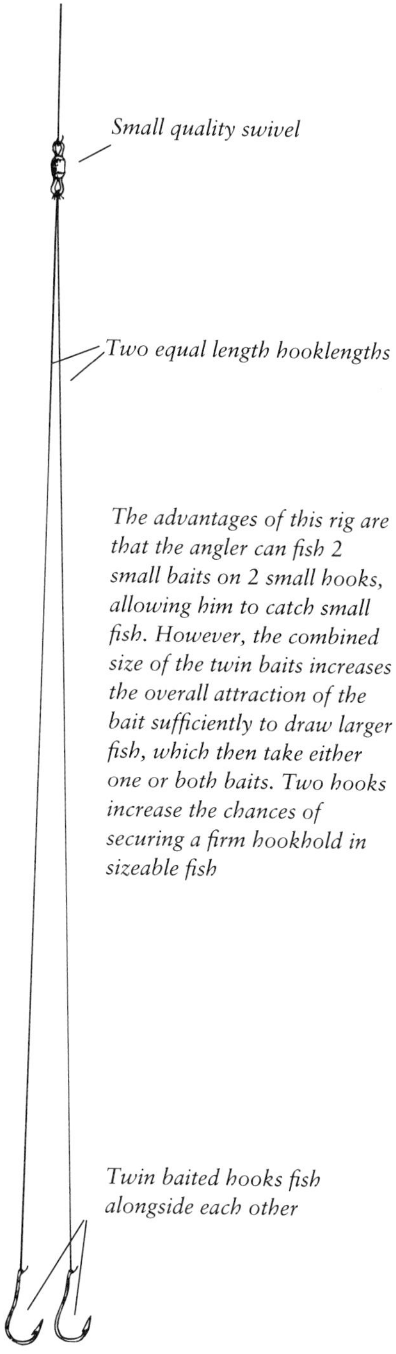

Fig. 13   Wishbone rig – can be
incorporated into most rigs.

Long-range casting is potentially very dangerous, with a risk of leads causing serious or even fatal injuries if they crack off during the initial inertia of the cast. Obviously, a shockleader is a must. But how do you fish a lead attached with a weak link at long range? The answer is really very simple. Instead of the lead being attached to a split oval or link, a loop of line (which must be at least 50lb BS for long range work) is tied at the bottom of the trace. The lead is then attached to this loop by about 4in of weaker line, about 10lb BS. The loop in the bottom of the trace is pushed through the eye on the lead, and it is held in position by a steel nail or a strong panel pin. Before it is secured, the pin is pushed through a small block of foam or polystyrene about ½in square. The pin securely holds the lead during the cast, but then falls free or floats out when the lead hits the water. This leaves the rig firmly anchored to the seabed, but should the lead become snagged, it is easily broken off. This system can be incorporated into almost any type of terminal rig (Fig. 14).

Fishing at range in shallow water and over rough ground is one of the most difficult situations that the shore angler can expect to meet, especially when there is a strong run of tide. Under these situations, the pulley rig comes into its own (Fig. 15). The basic principle of the pulley rig is that when a fish is hooked the weight of the fish draws the running part of the rig, with the lead attached to the end,

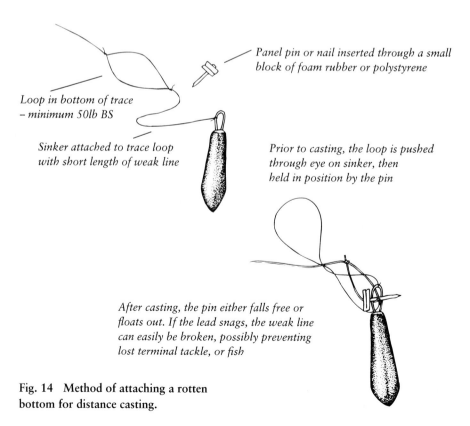

Panel pin or nail inserted through a small block of foam rubber or polystyrene

Loop in bottom of trace
– minimum 50lb BS

Sinker attached to trace loop with short length of weak line

Prior to casting, the loop is pushed through eye on sinker, then held in position by the pin

After casting, the pin either falls free or floats out. If the lead snags, the weak line can easily be broken, possibly preventing lost terminal tackle, or fish

Fig. 14 Method of attaching a rotten bottom for distance casting.

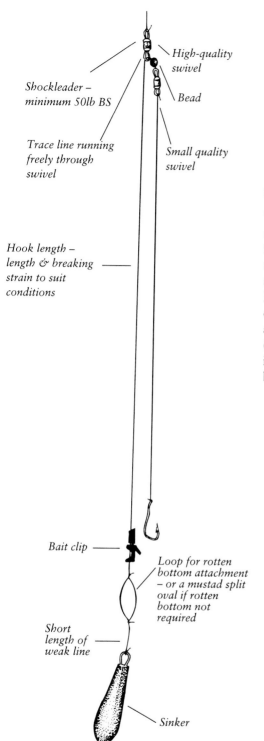

High-quality swivel

Shockleader – minimum 50lb BS

Bead

Trace line running freely through swivel

Small quality swivel

Hook length – length & breaking strain to suit conditions

Bait clip

Loop for rotten bottom attachment – or a mustad split oval if rotten bottom not required

Short length of weak line

Sinker

Fig. 15 Pulley rig for fishing at long range over rough/shallow ground.

through the swivel. When retrieving the fish the lead is held high in the water and not left hanging at the bottom of the trace, when there would be a strong risk of it snagging on the way in.

Short-range work

The beauty of many estuaries is that it is often possible to fish at short range. This is particularly advantageous for both novice and junior anglers. In its most simple form, short-range fishing involves little more than simply tying the hook on to the end of the line, then freelining a live prawn, a crab or a mackerel head (Fig. 16). This is a tremendously sporting technique for catching the likes of bass on light tackle. In other situations

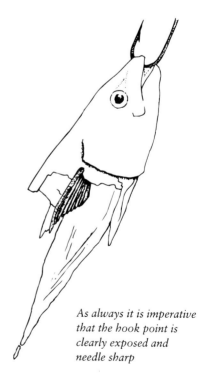

As always it is imperative that the hook point is clearly exposed and needle sharp

Fig. 16 Method of attaching a mackerel head and guts on to a hook.

37

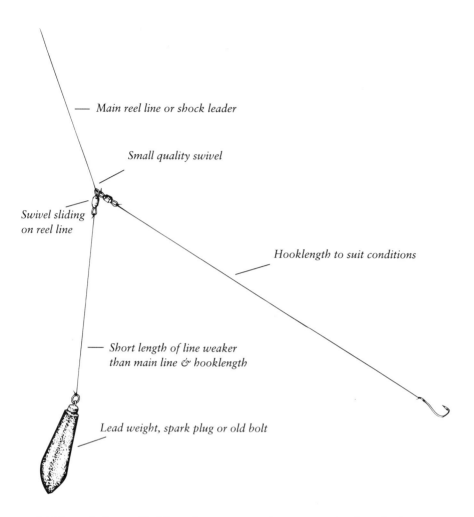

Main reel line or shock leader

Small quality swivel

Swivel sliding
on reel line

Hooklength to suit conditions

Short length of line weaker
than main line & hooklength

Lead weight, spark plug or old bolt

lobbing a bait out 40–50 yards or more
will be necessary.

Short-range rigs vary little from long-range rigs, although there will rarely be
a need to use bait clips. The paternoster
rig in its various forms is again a good
all-round choice, incorporating a rotten
bottom whenever required.

The running leger (Fig. 17) is another
alternative which is especially popular
with bass anglers as it allows fish to take
a bait against minimal resistance, thus
reducing the chance of spooking the fish.
A rotten bottom is easily incorporated
into a short-range running leger, simply
by attaching the lead to a swivel with a
short link of weak line. Without the
need of a powerful cast, rigs can be

**Fig. 17 Running leger for boat or shore
– rough ground.**

lobbed a fair distance without any risk
of a dangerous crack off.

The running paternoster (Fig. 18) is
an excellent rig for fishing at short range
into heavily weeded ground and, once
again, it can be tied with or without a
rotten bottom. The big advantage with
a running paternoster under these situations is that the lead can sink down
below the weed, leaving the bait lying on
top where it will be easier for fish to
locate.

Whenever fishing rough or weedy
ground it is important to use sufficient
lead to keep the bait static on the bottom.

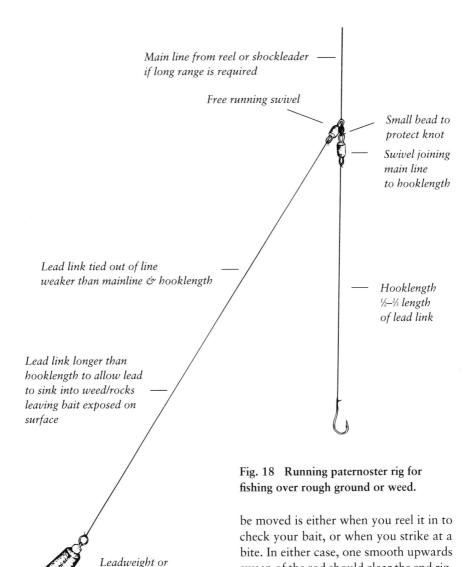

Main line from reel or shockleader —
if long range is required

Free running swivel

Small bead to
protect knot

Swivel joining
main line
to hooklength

Lead link tied out of line
weaker than mainline & hooklength —

Hooklength
½–⅔ length
of lead link

Lead link longer than
hooklength to allow lead
to sink into weed/rocks —
leaving bait exposed on
surface

Fig. 18 Running paternoster rig for fishing over rough ground or weed.

Leadweight or
old sparkplug
or bolt

If the tide or current is allowed to roll the rig around it will very quickly snag. After casting, it may be a great temptation to try and move the rig slightly 'just to see whether or not it is snagged': don't do it. The chances are that if it wasn't snagged before then it will be after you have dragged it. The first time the rig should be moved is either when you reel it in to check your bait, or when you strike at a bite. In either case, one smooth upwards sweep of the rod should clear the end rig, and hook the fish.

Fishing with a spoon from the shore

A spoon rig is a very effective technique to use either from a boat (see Chapter 5) or from the shore. The shore angler casts the rig out, then slowly inches it back across the bottom, when, hopefully, it will attract the attention of fish, and especially members of the flatfish family. Keeping the bait slowly moving is a prerequisite for success when using this technique – as it is in so many forms of estuary angling.

Float fishing

There are many situations where using a float in an estuary is an advantage, and floatfishing with light tackle will provide the angler with tremendous sport. The usual target species for the sea angler when floatfishing are mullet, pollack, bass, garfish, wrasse and mackerel.

Harbour walls, piers and rock marks giving access to deep water are the sort of places to consider using a float – or anywhere where the fish are likely to be within comfortable casting range. A float can also be a big advantage in situations when it is possible to trot the float along the course of a narrow channel or creek.

Many of the traditional 'sea floats' are huge polystyrene affairs, but now there are many more modern freshwater designs available in the tackle shops, which are far more effective and sensitive, and allow the use of more sporting tackle. The larger, more buoyant designs should not be totally dismissed, however, as they are useful when fishing very turbulent water, or when extra casting distance is necessary.

Most anglers tend to use the sliding float in the sea (Fig. 19). This is a float with the line running through the middle of the float's body. The trouble with some other methods, such as attaching the float bottom only 'waggler style', is that false bites, caused by the current or wave action dragging the float under, can be a constant problem. The sliding float is also the easiest type to rig for fishing depths greater than those that

can be comfortably cast with a float set at fixed depth. This is achieved by using a stop knot or a small piece of rubber band tied to the line.

A sliding float is rigged as follows. A small bead is threaded on to the main reel line, followed by the float. A drilled bullet, large enough to cock the float, is next, followed by a second bead and then a small swivel. The hooklength, generally between 3ft and 6ft is tied to the other end of this swivel. A bunch of split shot, instead of the bullet, may be preferable when using smaller freshwater floats, providing a higher degree of sensitivity. Note that it is now illegal to use lead shot in fresh water, and several non-toxic alternatives are available. As a general rule, if you require a rod licence in the area that you are fishing you should not use lead weights smaller than 2oz. If in doubt, seek advice from the local tackle shop or National Rivers Authority office, before you fish.

The stop knot or band is then tied at the required distance from the hook. Following casting, the weight steadily draws the line through the float until the top bead and the float come up against the stop knot, thus cocking the float.

The ideal tackle for fishing a float in the sea is either a long spinning rod or a freshwater carp or pike rod. Occasionally it may be possible to use a freshwater match rod, but in all cases a fixed spool reel is invariably the best reel to use, allowing far greater control of the terminal tackle than is possible with a multiplier. Some specialists favour the traditional centre pin reel, but these require a high degree of skill to use efficiently.

Fig. 19 **Simple sliding float rig for boat or shore.**

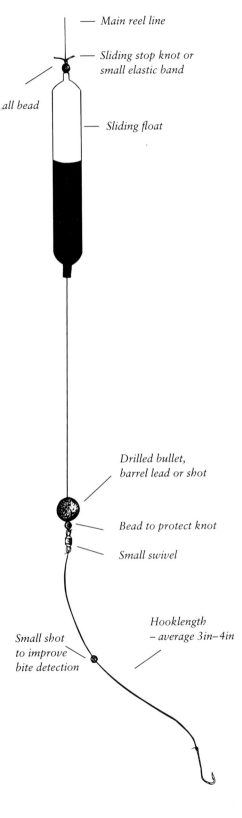

— Main reel line

— Sliding stop knot or
small elastic band

all bead

— Sliding float

Drilled bullet,
barrel lead or shot

Bead to protect knot

Small swivel

Hooklength
– average 3in–4in

Small shot
to improve
bite detection

Spinning

Spinning, and the use of lures in general, is an excellent way of exploring the coastline within an estuary. With a little practice it is possible to work a lure accurately and enticingly through systems of channels, around rock, through patches of weed or temptingly around pier pilings or boat moorings. Some of our finest salt-water sport fish, notably bass, mullet, pollack and coalfish, can be readily caught on lures.

Spinning is an active form of fishing, which is probably why it appeals to an increasing number of anglers. Whereas traditional bait fishing often involves long periods of inactivity punctuated by an occasional fish, the angler fishing lures will be constantly on the move. By travelling light it is possible to cover large areas of unfamiliar coastline, stopping here and there at interesting looking marks for a dozen or so casts before moving on.

The lure angler will be able to cover vast areas of water, which should also help to locate isolated populations of fish. By twitching and wobbling his lures in an enticing manner around partially submerged features, he will be hoping to induce a strike, either from a fish lying in wait hoping to ambush its prey, or from fish actively hunting. Several species of fish swim at varying depths of water, and a carefully controlled spinner can be made to cover all depths of water in order to find them.

One of the biggest advantages spinning has to offer is that trips can be planned at short notice, without having to rush out and purchase or dig bait. A minimal range of lures will last indefinitely, until they are ultimately lost in use. This allows the angler to spend the maximum amount of time actually

fishing. For many anglers this often involves snatching a couple of hours here and there at short notice.

A small selection of different types of lures will cope with most situations. Collecting lures can become addictive, but most are variations of two or three basic designs. Others seem to be designed to catch more anglers than fish! The most useful types of lures are spinners and spoons, plugs, and artificial sandeels (Fig. 20). But there is plenty of scope for fly fishing within an estuary and many of the American soft rubber worms and fish imitations are increasingly proving their worth.

Catching a few fish on lures involves little more than continually casting and retrieving the lure in the right place. The right place could be a deep channel, or across the actual mouth of the estuary, or maybe over a submerged reef or

Spinning for bass in an estuary at low water. Fish will be concentrated in a smaller volume of water, and results can be impressive, especially as the tide starts to flood.

weedbed. Working lures around pier or pontoon supports can be particularly productive, and sometimes even seemingly featureless stretches of open beach can produce fish. Continually casting and retrieving will catch a few fish, but, as in all angling, successful spinning requires a certain amount of technique.

In order to catch fish on spinners it is not necessary to cast out somewhere towards the horizon. Long casts can sometimes pay dividends, but fish will often be feeding within 25 yards of the shore, and a cast parallel to the beach might well prove more successful than one straight out to sea. By all means start by casting at long range, but do not be afraid to drop a few casts short. Always try to cover as much of an area as is possible.

A big mistake that many lure anglers make is they do not work their lures close enough to cover, which is normally where most of the target fish will be lurking. This is because they are scared of losing a few lures. Yet these same anglers are quite happy to consign £10-worth of

worms to the deep each trip. It is possible to fish lures over very rough ground without getting snagged, provided when you start the retrieve you raise the rod top and keep the lure moving.

With experience, lure losses can be kept at a minimum. Even 8lb BS line is

Fig. 20 Basic rig for casting artificial eels boat or shore.

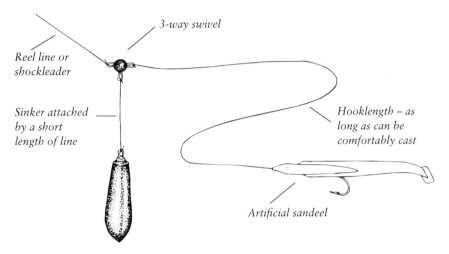

Reel line or shockleader

3-way swivel

Sinker attached by a short length of line

Hooklength – as long as can be comfortably cast

Artificial sandeel

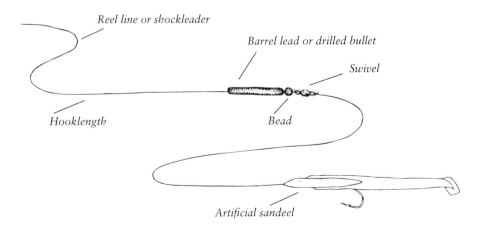

Reel line or shockleader

Barrel lead or drilled bullet

Swivel

Hooklength

Bead

Artificial sandeel

strong enough to pull a lure out of kelp with steadily applied pressure. Over very snaggy ground you could try using a heavier-breaking strain line to reduce losses, or substitute the standard treble hook for a single, which is less prone to catching rock and weed and is just as likely to secure a decent hook hold in the fish.

It is more important to carry a selection of different coloured lures than different types, not all colours of the rainbow, a basic range including a few silver and dark coloured lures should suffice. Personally I favour those lures that most closely resemble the fishes' natural prey, as opposed to some of the horrendously bright and gaudy creations often seen in tackle shops. I'm sure many of these work well on occasions, I am simply far more confident if I am using a lure that looks right.

The way that you actually retrieve your lure is where the real technique and experience with lure fishing starts to count. One day a lure slowly wobbling and twitching through the water will prompt take after take, the following day, and often at the same mark, only a fast and erratic retrieve brings results. Always strive to keep the lures action as interesting as possible. Frequent twitches of the rod top, stopping the retrieve for a second or two, altering the angle of retrieve, anything which helps maximize upon or improve the lure's attractiveness will help.

The sink and draw method is one of the best. Allow the lure to sink, then raise it sharply through the water with a combination of winding the reel and raising the rod top. Allow the lure to sink back again, and so on. At the end of the day it is down to you to convince the fish that it is not an unattractive lump of metal swimming through the water, but an injured baitfish, an easy prey and an easy meal.

5 Boat-fishing techniques

Uptiding

It was in the Thames Estuary back in the early 1970s when uptiding, or boatcasting as it is also known, was developed. With the realization that many species of fish are scared away from an anchored boat, by noises emitting from the boat's hull, or by the anchor warp and anglers on deck, a few forward-thinking anglers devised a method of effectively bottom fishing well away from the boat. This was found to be especially beneficial when fishing in shallow water – typical conditions that are found in estuaries.

It was found that not only were fish scared away from the immediate vicinity of the boat, but that on either side of the boat there was an area in which there was a higher concentration of fish than elsewhere. This was due to those fish that were swimming away from the area of disturbance joining the fish that were already swimming at a distance away

Fig. 21 Diagram showing reaction of fish as they approach an anchored boat.

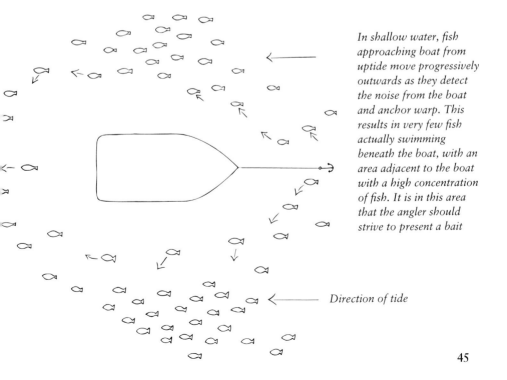

In shallow water, fish approaching boat from uptide move progressively outwards as they detect the noise from the boat and anchor warp. This results in very few fish actually swimming beneath the boat, with an area adjacent to the boat with a high concentration of fish. It is in this area that the angler should strive to present a bait

Direction of tide

from the boat (Fig. 21). It is here that the angler should strive to present his baits.

The actual distance that fish will swim away from a boat depends on several factors. Probably the most significant factor is the depth of the water, since there is a far greater degree of disturbance to fish in shallow water than in deeper water. It therefore follows that anglers should try to fish furthest away from the boat when the water is shallow, unless other seabed features such as gullies, sandbanks, mussel beds or wrecks, are present to influence the distribution of the fish.

Different species of fish react differently to noise disturbance. The shyer species, such as bass, tope and cod, are more likely to give a wider berth to the boat than more sedentary species such as rays.

One of the big advantages of uptiding is that it ensures that the angler's bait is where the majority of fish will be looking for it, hard on the seabed. When fishing in very strong or even moderate runs of tide (typically encountered within an estuary), many anglers simply drop their tackle to the seabed, re-engage the reel and fish happily away thinking they are fishing on the seabed. In fact the tide will probably have lifted the bait well up into mid-water.

Uptiding with grip leads ensures that the bait remains anchored to the seabed. But grip leads have a second important function. When a fish takes the bait and then tries to swim off, the resistance of the grip wires will more often than not set the hook far more effectively than most anglers can.

The classic uptide rig is once again the simple running leger which will cope perfectly well in most situations. I always use short plastic tubi-type booms to carry the lead, finding the extra length helps to prevent the hooklength tangling on grip wires during casting, especially when casting into the wind.

The hooklength should be 3–5 ft in length. When targeting smaller fish, such as flatties, use light breaking strains of nylon, but use stronger line when fishing for cod, smooth hounds, rays, etc. Often it's not just the fish you will be fighting, but the tide as well. Wire will be needed for hooklengths when fishing for tope or conger.

The actual length of the hooklength is very important. When fishing at slack water or when there is little run of tide, a long hooklength can help to move a bait enticingly over the seabed. However, in a strong run of tide, a bait fished off a long hooklength can be lifted well off the bottom, and away from feeding fish. In these cases a short hooklength, perhaps 3–4 ft in length, will be far more efficient.

In most cases, it is essential to use a shockleader when uptiding, certainly if there is any risk of leads cracking off and causing injuries or damage. A lot of weed or other debris floating in the tide after flooding upstream can clog on a shockleader knot and then jam in the tip ring, possibly risking a lost fish. Under these circumstances using 25lb BS or heavier line straight through will solve the knot problem, but extreme care should be made when casting. Also, the stronger the line, the thicker the line diameter, creating more surface area of line for the tide to pull against, usually necessitating the need for heavier leads.

There is another reason for using a shockleader when uptiding. The strains on the reel line are massive when a decent fish is hooked in a strong tide, and a lot of very big fish are lost on the surface. A

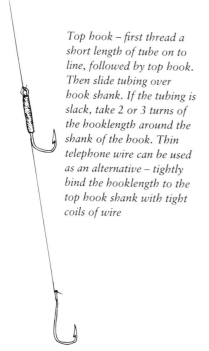

Top hook – first thread a short length of tube on to line, followed by top hook. Then slide tubing over hook shank. If the tubing is slack, take 2 or 3 turns of the hooklength around the shank of the hook. Thin telephone wire can be used as an alternative – tightly bind the hooklength to the top hook shank with tight coils of wire

Bottom hook – tied on as normal

Fig. 22   Pennel rig for optimum bait presentation with big baits.

shockleader can help prevent such losses. With the security of a couple of turns of heavy leader line on the reel the angler can help the netsman by holding the fish against the pull of the tide. But a leader is no substitute for an accurately set clutch, and is no excuse for the angler to bully fish into the net.

The type and size of grip lead should be chosen to cope with the strength of tide. Ideally, the angler should use the lightest practical weight that he can cast the required distance, and which will then hold bottom. Breakout-type leads, such as the excellent Gemini system, are perfect, and allow fish to trip the wires when they move off, usually setting the

hook in the process. In very strong runs of tide, a lead with fixed grip wires might well be necessary. Long tail and grip wires will have a tendency to lie flat on the seabed and improve grip when the tide is pulling at its hardest.

Bait presentation is just as important when uptiding as in any other form of fishing. The added problems the angler should allow for when uptiding, are the force of casting, and tide. Both can easily destroy a badly prepared bait, possibly masking the hookpoint in the process, and resulting in lost fish.

The presentation of most baits can be improved with a couple of turns of fine bait elastic to hold them secure on the hook. The pennel rig is invaluable in many uptiding situations (Fig. 22). As well as helping to maintain decent bait presentation, it has the advantage of having a second hook to take hold. It is good practice to hang the bait on one of the lead's grip wires prior to casting. This not only makes casting a lot easier and a lot safer, but helps to minimize damage to carefully prepared baits.

Other tricks to assist bait presentation are the addition of thin strips of squid or fish on to the hooks. These serve to keep the hook points clear and exposed, add to the overall attractiveness of the bait, and, in coloured water, act as additional attractors which help advertize the location of the bait. When using worms, tightly thread and bunch them on to the hooks (Fig. 23). Loose worms are easily ripped off during casting, and easily pecked away by small fish.

The basic principle of uptiding is that the lead is cast up and across the tide. The lead is allowed to sink swiftly to the bottom, to allow the grip lead to take hold, and then a belly of slack line is let out into the tide to further assist the

Always ensure the hook points are not masked by bait. This will increase baits: fish hooked ratio. A small strip of squid on each hook helps achieve this and adds to attraction

Fig. 23 Method of mounting lugworm on a pennel rig.

lead hold firm. The rod tip consequently bends over into the tide. With so much line out, it is rare for the angler to see the first delicate taps when a fish finds the bait: which, considering the impatience of many anglers, is often no bad thing!

The first indication of a bite is generally a couple of delicate nods of the tip, which are no indication of the size of fish. Then, depending on the strength of tide, size of fish, and efficiency of the grip leads, the nodding will either continue, or the lead will break out, causing the tip to spring smartly upright, with slack line drifting downtide. In either case the angler does *not* strike. Pick the rod up and quickly wind in all slack line. Wind until you feel the solid resistance of the fish on the end, and then lean firmly into the fish to set the hook.

If the fish has not broken the lead out, the initial drill is the same. When the lead is felt, the angler should firmly break it out, very quickly winding to retrieve any extra slack until the fish is

felt. Only then, lean into the fish to set the hook.

The other classic application of boat-casting is when the angler casts up and across the tide using a plain lead just heavy enough to drag steadily or roll across the bottom in the tide. The boat is anchored within casting range of a fish-holding feature, usually a sand bar or a gully, when the angler casts the bait uptide of the feature. The plain lead steadily drags across the feature, where the bait will hopefully be intercepted by a fish. This method lends itself greatly towards using spoons and other artificial attractors, including artificial sandeels which can also be very effectively fished using an uptider (Fig. 24).

For many anglers the biggest benefit that uptiding has to offer is that it allows the pursuit of some of our most sporting species of fish on light tackle. Big cod, rays, bass, tope and smooth hounds can all be fished, using a light rod and a light line, under conditions that, until the development of uptiding, would either have been impossible to fish, or required short stocky boat rods, heavy line and horrendous lumps of lead, killing the sporting qualities of all but the biggest fish.

Downtiding

Many anglers consider downtiding as almost a second rate sport in comparison to the increasing popularity of uptiding. Yet, when practised correctly, down-tiding requires as much and perhaps even more skill than uptiding.

The time to consider downtiding is when the depth of water restricts the effectiveness of uptiding. The actual depth at which uptiding becomes impractical varies according to the strength of the tide, but I rarely uptide in more than 75ft of water, except when there is very little run of tide.

The real skill in downtiding is in constantly maintaining bottom contact. After all, the majority of fish in this country are essentially bottom feeders. Many anglers who recognize the fact that their baits are getting lifted away from the bottom by the tide simply add an extra couple of ounces of lead. As well as reducing the sporting potential from catching small to average fish, large leads are not always the best way of ensuring a bait remains on the seabed. There are several factors which play a big part in dictating how easy it is to hold bottom.

Fig. 24 How to fish a sandbank or gulley from an anchored position adjacent to the bank.

Most estuaries experience a twice-daily tidal cycle, namely two high and two low water periods within any one 24-hour period. The strength at which the tide runs during the six hours between these four slack water periods varies considerably. Even so it is usually the middle third of the tide, the two hours in the middle of the six, that experiences the strongest tidal flow, and with the ebb tide usually considerably stronger than the flood tide.

It is therefore common sense that different amounts of lead will be required to keep a bait on the bottom at different stages of the tide; but the breaking strain of the line is also important. As the breaking strain of the line increases, so does the diameter of that line (more so in the case of lower quality lines than modern hi-tech lines that are available today). As the line diameter increases, so does the surface area of the line, and

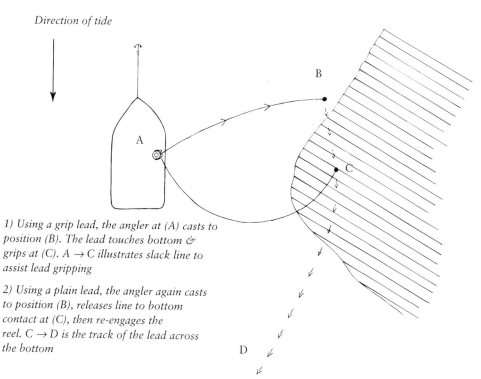

Direction of tide

1) *Using a grip lead, the angler at (A) casts to position (B). The lead touches bottom & grips at (C). A → C illustrates slack line to assist lead gripping*

2) *Using a plain lead, the angler again casts to position (B), releases line to bottom contact at (C), then re-engages the reel. C → D is the track of the lead across the bottom*

consequently the amount of drag exerted by the tidal flow. Common sense tells us that with more surface area of line beneath the water more lead will be required to keep, say, a 25lb BS line in the same spot downtide of the boat, than a 15lb BS line from the same manufacturer.

During extreme deep water and strong tide situations, wire line is often a better choice than monofilament. The big advantage with wire is that its diameter is much less than monofilament of an equivalent BS. Another big plus with using wire in deep water situations is it has little stretch, resulting in far greater bite sensitivity at the rod.

Recent years have seen a lot of modern braided lines come on to the market, more or less high tech versions of the old dacron. Early reports on the effectiveness of these products are very encouraging. At the moment, however, the high cost of these lines remains a deterrent to most anglers, but an increase in market demand might well be reflected in lower prices.

Fig. 25 Diagram explaining how to trot baits downtide towards fish concentrated around any special feature.

The actual shape and type of lead the angler is using can also make a big difference. Traditionally, anglers fished downtide using flat bottom, cone-shaped leads, and in many ways these are still a good choice as they sit firmly on the bottom. Bomb-shaped or rounded leads have a tendency to roll about. Often it may be desirable to allow a lead to roll about, as under the right conditions a bait rolling around in the tide, matched with an angler who is in control of the situation, will outfish a static bait.

Some anglers fish downtide using grip leads, in much the same way as other anglers fish uptide. First they drop the lead to the sea bed, then release a bow of line, just as when uptiding. In this case the bow of line lies in a vertical plane, passing over the top of and then downtide of the lead. Bite sensitivity is obviously reduced when using this technique, but most fish hook themselves when breaking the leads out.

Even though I have stressed that the biggest problem confronted by anglers when they are downtiding is maintaining contact with the bottom, the real art of downtiding is in allowing the baited rig to trot steadily back with the tide (Fig. 25). This ensures a far greater area of

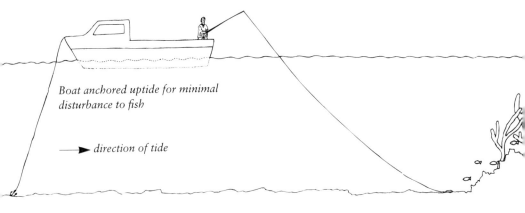

Boat anchored uptide for minimal disturbance to fish

➤ *direction of tide*

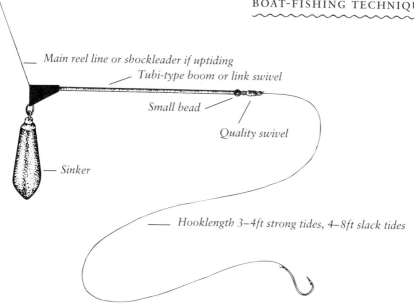

Main reel line or shockleader if uptiding

Tubi-type boom or link swivel

Small bead

Quality swivel

Sinker

Hooklength 3–4ft strong tides, 4–8ft slack tides

Fig. 26 **Running leger for general boat fishing.**

the seabed is covered than when using a static bait. The big advantage with this method is that it locates any isolated pockets of fish astern of the boat, especially when the boat is anchored uptide of the actual feature, which might be a reef, sand bar or even a wreck.

In order for downtiding to be employed to its maximum potential, it is important that the angler holds his rod at all times. The reel should be left in free spool, the angler slowly allowing the bait to trot back with the tide. This is achieved by occasionally lifting the rod tip and releasing a few yards of line, always confirming that the bait is on the bottom by carefully tapping the lead on the seabed.

A single-hook running leger will suffice for most downtiding situations (Fig. 26). The simplest way to tie a running leger is to use a good sliding boom. I used to use short stubby booms such as zip sliders for the bulk of my downtide boat rigs, but in recent years I have increasingly used longer booms of about 4in, which greatly reduce the risk of

tangling on the descent by keeping the hooklength well clear of the main line.

The boom is threaded on to the line first, followed by a small bead to protect the knot. A small quality swivel such as a Berkley or Mustad is used to attach the hooklength to the main line. When I require a second or third hook I use one of the excellent Mustad/Knotless paternoster booms, which can be attached and removed from the trace quickly at will. Another option is the wishbone rig, a good choice for fishing for flatties but when there is a possibility of catching a bigger fish such as a cod or a bass.

Finally, when choosing the actual length of the hooklength, the target species and tidal flow are the things to consider. A long hooklength, in excess of 6ft is a good choice in light to moderate tides. It will allow the flow of water to impart a lot of movement into the bait. But a strong tide can lift a long hooklength off the bottom and clear of the fish, defeating the whole object of the exercise. In strong tides, reduce the length of hooklength to below 6ft, to ensure that baits remain on the seabed.

Fishing on the drift

Fishing from a drifting boat is an excellent method of presenting a bait or lure. It is often necessary to cover as much ground as possible in order to locate isolated pockets of feeding fish. Drifting over clean ground can look deceptively easy. The angler's prime objective is always to ensure contact with the bottom at all times – the vast majority of our fish species are bottom feeders and baits trailing in mid-water will catch few fish. It is generally possible to use light tackle when drifting; tackle heavier than 12lb or 20lb class is rarely required.

The ideal end rig is, again, the simple running leger, with hooklength up to 6ft – often longer when drifting for plaice. A decent boom of about 4in will help keep the rig tangle free and assist bait presentation.

The choice and size of lead is very important. You will need just enough weight to keep the rig on the bottom, but not so much that it overloads the rod. The old-fashioned, circular, studded watch leads are ideal. Some anglers claim that they kick up little puffs of sand as they drag across the seabed, helping to attract the fish. The addition of an attractor spoon on the hooklength, about 6in from the baited hook, is popular when fishing for plaice and other species of flatfish (Fig. 27).

With practice, keeping the bait on the bottom when drifting is easy. The bait should be lowered over the side of the boat, facing away from the direction of the drift to avoid the line dragging back under the boat's keel. Lower the bait to the bottom slowly to prevent the long hooklength spinning back around the main line; this is where a decent boom is a benefit.

When you feel the lead tap on the bottom do not immediately re-engage the reel, but use your thumb to steadily check the line running off the spool. A small multiplier is a far better choice than a fixed spool for this sort of fishing. Release a little more line, then, with the spool checked, slightly raise the rod tip and lower it to confirm the bait is still on the bottom. If it is not on the bottom release a little more line. This process is continually repeated throughout the drift, with the baited rig getting further and further behind the boat.

If a bite is felt do not strike straight away, but release a few yards of line to avoid moving the baited hook away from the fish. After about a minute check the line leaving the spool with your thumb, and if a fish is there you should feel either a rattle on the rod tip, or the rod will slowly bend over against the resistance caused by the weight of the fish. Re-engage the spool, wind in any slack, and with one steady movement raise the rod, winding the reel at the same time to set the hook.

Drifting over rough ground is far more demanding. The running leger rig is again useful, but a paternoster, with the baits above the weight, can be a better choice. When using the paternoster it is a good idea to fish the lead off a weak line, which will hopefully restrict any tackle losses to just the lead. Shorter hook snoods will reduce snags. The other alternative is a running leger rig with the lead dangling from a short length of weak line which will act as a very efficient rotten bottom if the lead gets snagged.

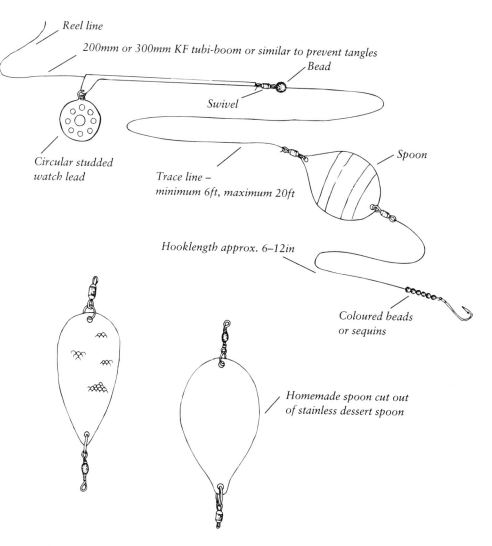

Reel line

200mm or 300mm KF tubi-boom or similar to prevent tangles

Bead

Swivel

Circular studded
watch lead

Trace line –
minimum 6ft, maximum 20ft

Spoon

Hooklength approx. 6–12in

Coloured beads
or sequins

Homemade spoon cut out
of stainless dessert spoon

The prime consideration when drifting over rough ground (unlike clean ground) is to avoid baits trailing behind the boat. It is important to maintain as near a vertical line as possible between the rod tip and the end rig to avoid baits

Fig. 27 Spoon rig for fishing on the drift or boatcasting.

being dragged into snags, and it is often necessary to use an extra couple of ounces of lead.

53

6 Fish species

Bass

Next to cod, the bass must rank as our most sought-after sea fish. Certainly it is one of the most beautiful, perfectly proportioned in every aspect. For many anglers the European sea bass epitomizes everything that a fish should be. On light tackle the bass can be relied upon to provide tremendous sport, furthermore it is also one of the finest eating fish in the sea – what more could the angler ask of a fish?

At some time or other bass can be caught in almost any marine environment, ranging from shallow surf beaches and sand banks to deep water wrecks and reefs, many miles offshore; estuaries are noted bass venues.

Like so many other sea fish, the bass is drawn into estuaries by the abundance of natural food. But for this species the sheltered water environment of many estuaries serves another very important purpose, since they are nursery areas for juvenile bass; indeed many are now designated as conservation areas where fishing for bass is either totally banned or restricted to certain times of the year.

Commercial pressure over far too many years has dramatically reduced British bass stocks to a shadow of what they once were, but the signs for the future are encouraging. A series of warm summers and mild winters throughout the late eighties and early nineties have provided ideal breeding conditions for bass. The result is large numbers of young bass; fish up to about 2½lb are now common in many parts of the country. More and more anglers are now catching bass – which at times can be regarded as a nuisance when targeting other species.

With such a high price tag on their heads it has not taken long for the more unscrupulous rod and line fishermen (I refuse to use the word anglers) to fish deliberately for young bass solely for financial gain. Not only is this totally deplorable, but in many cases it is highly illegal, as many have found out to their cost; fines are hefty. The minimum landing size for bass is 14in in length, measured from the tip of the snout to the end of the tail fin. Any bass below this length must be returned immediately to the sea.

It used to be widely quoted that bass could not be caught north of a line drawn from Anglesey to the Wash. Today this is far from the truth and bass can be caught anywhere in the UK, including the far north of Scotland. A few years ago I set myself the target of catching a bass from England, Ireland, Wales and Scotland in the same season, and succeeded. The Scottish bass, or so I thought, would be the hardest challenge, but I caught two out of a total catch of five at my very first attempt – and they were not taken on the border either, but at Dunnet Bay in

Caithness, about 20 miles to the west of John o'Groats!

It also used to be generally regarded that bass could only be caught between the spring and autumn. By and large this still has a degree of truth in it, but in many of the more southern estuaries bass are now regularly caught throughout the year, especially during the more mild

Many estuaries are nursery areas for small bass. This beautiful little fish took a king ragworm. Always treat small fish with care and return them to the water as soon as possible.

winters. Some of the biggest bass of the year are taken in late autumn, and many are caught in and around estuaries.

The natural diet of the bass is wide ranging, and the fish can be caught on more or less anything, depending on the time of the year. Peeler crab, fish, squid, worms, prawns, livebaits, and a whole range of lures all regularly catch bass. Some baits tend to be both more productive and more selective than others, consistently sorting out the better-quality fish.

Big bass like big baits, and their favourite is the head and guts from a mackerel or herring. More specimen bass are caught on fish baits than any other. Whole squid is also very successful, but for some reason the success of squid tends to be localized, mainly restricted to marks in the south. Peeler crab is certainly one of the most reliable baits, either the common green shore crab or, better still, an edible or velvet swimming crab. Livebaits are also popular with specimen bass. Pouting, whiting, poor cod and, of course, sandeels all make excellent baits, as do prawns. Livebaits should either be freelined or fished in conjunction with a float.

Lure fishing for bass has attained almost cult status in recent years. Although not always as successful as bait fishing, lure fishing provides tremendous sport, allowing the use of the lightest tackle. For general spinning, almost any sort of spoon or spinner will catch bass, but artificial rubber sandeels can be deadly. It is often the smaller sizes that catch both the most and the biggest fish.

Plugs have become very popular in recent years. Floating plugs are excellent for fishing shallow, rocky or heavily weeded ground which can be more or less impossible to fish with sinking lures.

The most successful types are made by Rapala and Rebel and are usually jointed, measuring 3½–5in in length. The action on these lures is an extremely realistic mimic of a sandeel.

In order to catch bass consistently it is important to carry out a lot of ground-work, and this means studying the intended mark thoroughly before you fish. Bass show a distinct preference for certain features, as opposed to open featureless expanses of sand and mud, but that is not to say they cannot be caught in such open places.

Look for distinct channels, and patches of rock and weed, regardless of how small and insignificant these might first appear. Even the tiniest patch of rock or kelp will have its resident population of crabs, prawns and other attractive food items. Bass know this, and it is highly likely that they will pay them a visit at some stage during each tide. Wooden groynes, old piers, pieces of wreckage and breakwaters all provide food and shelter for countless small fishes and crustaceans – a well-stocked larder for the bass.

Streams entering the main channel are another excellent place to present a bait. It is often said that bass like fresh water, and, although at times they are highly tolerant of brackish conditions, I personally feel that this association with fresh water has a more logical explanation. Wherever a stream enters the main channel of an estuary, or runs across an otherwise exposed beach, there will nearly always be a natural food trap in the form of a depression cut out by the action of the water. In addition, streams also carry certain items of food, as well as being attractive to many small fish and other forms of life.

Offshore, the sand bars at the mouth of an estuary are excellent places to fish for bass. Sandeels are abundant over many tidal sandbars and banks, and draw bass like a magnet. Deep depressions, carved out by the tide, will also be worth fishing, along with any of the features mentioned earlier.

When fishing for bass from either a boat or the shore, the need for stealth cannot be over-emphasized. Bass are cautious by nature and easily frightened. Fishing at dawn and dusk or at night will nearly always be more successful than during daylight, as bass tend to be far more active then than during broad daylight.

The optimum times to fish for bass are immediately following a spell of rough weather, which will have churned up the seabed, thus dislodging many items of food. Start fishing at low water, and fish the flooding tide up to high water. Once the tide starts to ebb within an estuary fish can still be caught, but the majority of fish tend to drop quickly back to deeper and more saline conditions as soon as the tide turns.

Cod

The cod is the most popular salt-water species of fish with British anglers. With their national distribution, cod are also one of the finest eating fish in the sea. On light and well-balanced tackle cod fight extremely well and, with an average size of 2–7lb it's not hard to see just why cod are such a popular species. That said, the numbers of cod in many parts of the country has been drastically reduced by intense overfishing. Thankfully there are still reasonable numbers of fish in many parts of the country.

Cod enter estuaries at certain times of the year in order to feed, and invariably

The mud-splattered face of this prime codling is a dead give-away that the fish has been caught within an estuary.

Right The smile says it all! A local angler with a respectable catch of codling from Redwick in South Wales. Fish are attracted to this area by large numbers of prawns.

whenever cod move into a particular area it is because they want to cash in on some locally abundant food item. For example, on or around the last set of spring tides in August, large numbers of cod and codling migrate towards Redwick, Magor and Goldcliff, at the eastern end of the Bristol Channel. They are drawn by the multitude of prawns that thrive in the area.

By November the numbers of prawns will have been drastically reduced, and the majority of fish start to drop back down the channel towards Cardiff and

Penarth, where they feed on a mixed and varied diet including crabs, marine worms and various species of small fish. Then, in mid-November, huge shoals of sprats arrive in the channel, and overnight the cod will again switch feeding habits, feeding on little else except sprats.

Similar feeding patterns are displayed at many other venues around the country, often at different times of the year, and often to cash in on different food supplies. The cod is a creature of habit and, based on past results, experienced anglers can often forecast the optimum tides well in advance.

The weather can and frequently does throw a spanner in the works, disrupting well-established migratory patterns. To illustrate this point I will return to the Bristol Channel. If we have a particularly wet summer and autumn the many rivers which flow into the eastern channel flood. Millions upon millions of gallons of fresh water pour into the estuary each day. This results in drastically reduced salinity levels and often increased pollution levels in the tidal waters east of Cardiff. This tends to keep the main head of fish well to the west until conditions improve.

If, as has happened in recent years, we then get a prolonged cold snap with persistent easterly winds, the fish can appear to vanish off the face of the earth. There will nearly always be an odd fish or two about for the boat angler to catch, but, by and large, the shore angler can expect many difficult sessions under such conditions. All around the country normally reliable and predictable movements of cod can be disrupted by seasonal factors. But the fact remains that cod are perfectly at home within the confines of many estuaries, where they can be relied on to provide outstanding sport.

Catching cod is not difficult, indeed at times it can be ridiculously easy to net a fish or two. That well-known saying of 'using the right bait, in the right place and at the right time' could very well have been coined by a keen cod angler. There will always be the odd angler who flukes a fish, but if many so-called fluke catches were seriously analysed it would be seen that the angler had inadvertently given the cod exactly what they wanted at the time, and not simply what most anglers 'assumed' they wanted. Let me give you an example.

Cod are fierce, predatory fish which feed heavily on small fish such as immature whiting, pouting and poor cod. Let's suppose that an angler was fishing a venue for codling, using smallish hooks baited with worm – not, you would agree, the best tactics for sorting out fighting fit double figure cod.

Eventually the angler hooks a 4in whiting, which totally fails to register at a distance of 120 yards on his stiff rod tip. Suddenly the rod bucks and lurches forward out of the rod rest, and after a five-minute struggle a 12lb cod is slapping about on the shingle! Everyone labels the fish a fluke, which technically I suppose it is. But that 4in whiting was prime big cod bait, and far more appealing to a 12-pounder than a washed-out blow lug. The only flukey part of the capture was that a size 1 fine-wired Aberdeen hook managed to secure a firm enough hold long enough to land the fish!

Cod are greedy feeders and small, washed out unappetizing baits are unlikely to appeal. Several big, fresh, and juicy worms, threaded up the hook shank, a whole squid or two, a decent lump of prime peeler crab, a half dozen mussels gently lashed on to the hook with fine elastic, a whole 6in razorfish and, of course, livebaits; these are the sort of baits that consistently score with decent cod.

With the exception of live baits, cod locate their food by using their highly developed sense of smell – how else are they going to find food in the often heavily coloured waters of estuaries? But even in a modest run of tide the juiciest bait will very quickly get washed out, and I can only continue to emphasize the importance of fishing quality baits. Twenty minutes is the absolute maximum that any bait should be left unchecked. Freshening up baits every 15 minutes or even less is a far more reliable policy. Cocktail baits often fish very well for cod, notably crab/rag, lug/squid, crab/squid and lug/razorfish – as long as it's big and fresh, hungry cod will be able to locate and then eat it.

Traces incorporating a pennel rig are invariably the best to use for cod, both afloat and ashore. The pennel rig makes presenting large baits far easier than if using single hook rigs, with the added bonus of extra hooking power. Many cod anglers stick to using a single fixed paternoster rig from the shore, and the running leger from a boat. Grip leads not only help to hold baits in the required position on the seabed, but they provide a firm anchoring point against which many cod will effectively hook themselves, as they engulf a bait and try to swim off with it.

The self-hooking livebait rig is one

particularly effective for very large cod. A smallish hook suspended below a larger hook, on a short length of line is baited with a piece of worm or fish, intended to tempt a small livebait. The angler casts the rig out, hoping that a small fish will quickly hang itself on to the small hook, and will frantically flap about trying to free itself.

The theory is that when a large fish such as a cod takes the small fish, the cod also engulfs the larger hook. It is exactly the same strategy that carp anglers adopt when fishing a boilie off a hair rig; a sprat to catch a mackerel so to speak. Obviously the angler will not always be sure he or she has hooked a livebait so there will be an element of chance with

A well-conditioned double-figure cod caught in the Bristol Channel by Andrew Leaves. Note the bait hanging from the fish's mouth: peeler crab, a deadly bait for cod.

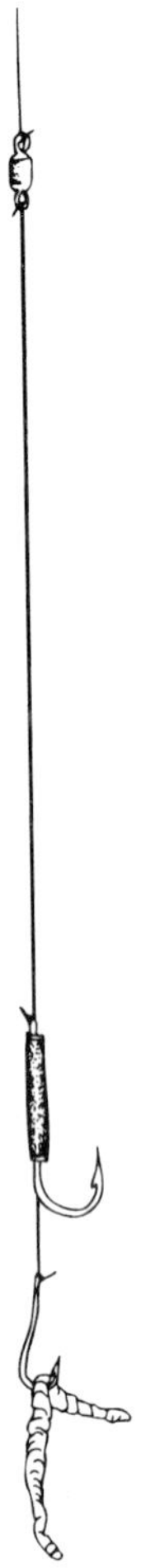

A small hook is beneath a larger hook, and baited with a small strip of fish or worms. The baitfish, usually whiting or pouting, get snared on the small hook, and start struggling. This attracts a larger fish, which engulfs the baitfish and hopefully the larger top hook as well. Always an element of chance, this is an ideal rig to try at long range on a second rod

Fig. 28 Self-hooking livebait rig.

this method. It is an excellent method to use with a second rod (Fig. 28).

Nearly all cod fishing afloat within estuaries is carried out at anchor, and uptiding is nearly always the most effective technique when conditions are suitable. It is possible to use the self-hooking livebait rigs afloat, but, without the need to cast baits as far as the shore angler, many boat anglers first catch their livebait, mount it correctly on to a hook and then either cast it uptide or fish it down-

tide by trotting it well astern of the boat. Which method is adopted will ultimately depend on the conditions on the day.

Dogfish

There are two species of dogfish commonly found in and around estuaries: the lesser-spotted and greater-spotted, the former being by far the most numerous. The lesser-spotted dogfish has an average weight of 1–2lb and is particularly abundant in many areas. It is often regarded as a nuisance, but many a potentially blank day has been saved by a doggie or two. The greater-spotted dogfish, also known as the bull huss, assumes much larger proportions. Fish weighing well into double figures are common.

Both species are most numerous throughout the spring, summer and autumn in the south and west, although they are caught on occasions off the east coast. Of the two, the lesser-spotted dogfish has the highest tolerance of brackish conditions, and is frequently caught in the upper reaches of estuaries where it shows no apparent discomfort if the water is heavily coloured. The greater-spotted dogfish favours the cleaner water and higher salinity levels found towards the mouth of the estuary and in the open sea.

Both species are scavengers, more so in the case of the lesser-spotted dogfish. They feed on a wide variety of natural food, but mainly on small crustaceans, shellfish and small fish. Various types of fish bait are invariably the best, especially chunks of sandeels. It is interesting to note that baits that have previously been frozen are often far more effective than fresh baits. Peeler crab, worms and squid also work well.

Neither species fight particularly well,

Proof enough that big cod are caught in many estuaries. The angler is Tony Kortens, the fish weighed almost 20lb, and was caught about half a mile offshore near Barry in South Wales. Many of the biggest cod are caught on livebaits.

but a decent greater-spotted dogfish is more than capable of putting a satisfying bend in a rod. The biggest problem that most anglers encounter with dogfish is unhooking them. Both these species have a nasty habit of wrapping their tails around the wrist and forearm and inflicting a nasty graze with their very rough skin. This is easily prevented by first grasping the tail, then taking a firm grip next to the fish's head while you remove the hook.

Flounder

The flounder is the classic fish of the estuary. With its nationwide distribution, the flounder has perhaps the strongest tolerance of fresh water of all of our saltwater species of fish. Indeed, the flounder is often caught well above the limit of salt-water influence and into pure fresh water by freshwater anglers targeting the likes of roach, chub or barble. That said, it is generally just the smaller specimens that venture this far inland, the larger fish certainly favour the more brackish and saline conditions found towards the mouth of the estuary.

The optimum time of the year for catching flounders in estuaries varies considerably, depending on their location. Many estuaries have sizeable populations of flounder throughout the spring and summer months, while fish at other venues peak during the autumn when they often feed voraciously, putting on body weight prior to spawning out at sea in the first few months of the year. The largest specimens, which include the current British records, are invariably caught during the autumn and early winter in the rivers of South Devon and Cornwall, such as the Teign, Exe, and Fowey.

The shore angler's choice of tackle and tactics to catch flounder will vary from venue to venue. With a fish whose average size does not commonly exceed 2½lb, it is preferable to use the lightest tackle practical in order to get the maximum amount of sport from each fish.

No giant, but a typical estuary flounder, caught by former English International angler Terry Thomas.

On the small rivers, or at times of little flow on the larger rivers, catching flounders on light to medium spinning tackle can be tremendous fun. But often it is necessary to use more substantial tackle, especially on the larger estuaries when there is a lot of weed or other debris floating about.

Various permutations of the running leger rig are the usual choice of terminal tackle. Like all members of the flatfish family, flounders are attracted by colour and movement, so there is plenty of scope for experimentation with various types of spoons, beads and other artificial attractors. Movement is probably more important than colour, and a bait that is slowly rolling across the bottom will nearly always attract more bites than a static bait.

Other methods which are sometimes used with great success for flounders include float fishing and spinning with a baited spinner. Float fishing is a useful method for working a bait slowly along the edge of a groyne or wall or perhaps through a deep channel, and provided the bait is on or within a few inches of the seabed, it can be a very effective method.

Spinning for flounders is a method not commonly seen these days (Fig. 29). The best types of spinner to use are bar spoons, such as a Mepps. The spinner's standard treble hook is first removed, then replaced with a single hook, usually a fine wired, long shank Aberdeen hook. Sometimes the hook is attached about an inch behind the main body of the spinner with a length of line or light wire. The hook is then baited, cast out, and slowly retrieved across the bottom. When a fish is felt nibbling at the bait the angler should slow down but continue the retrieve, making no attempt to strike; the fish will normally hook itself.

From a boat, the angler will be faced with a choice of either fishing on the drift or at anchor. Drifting is the classic technique for catching flounders afloat in an estuary. But where the current is particularly fast, or when drifting is impractical due to hazards to navigation, anchoring might be the better, not to mention safer, option. In both cases the angler's primary objective should be to keep baits on the move. The real beauty with fishing afloat is that it is usually possible to use far lighter tackle than would be required from the shore.

The standard treble hook is removed and replaced with a pair of fine wire hooks, mounted in tandem on to a length of about 25lb BS nylon. Baited with small ragworm, this is a deadly method for thin-lipped mullet, flounders & many other species

Fig. 29 Baited spinner rig.

By far the most successful all-round bait for flounder is peeler crab. More specimen fish have fallen to crab baits than any other. All types of marine worms also make excellent baits, notably harbour ragworm and lug. However, worm baits rarely remain intact and effective for long, given the attention of crabs. Small thin strips of mackerel or other fish can also work well on occasions, especially a fillet from the side of a sandeel, or even a small, whole sandeel. Fish is a good flounder bait in the lower reaches of the estuary. In the upper reaches of the estuary, in brackish water or following flooding, garden worms can often be used with some success.

Mullet

For many years mullet were considered more or less uncatchable on rod and line, and many of the older sea angling books proudly proclaimed this fact. Furthermore, they usually went on to state that this was due to the fact that mullet have very soft mouths and fed mainly on minute particles and seaweed. Today we know this to be far from the truth, and mullet are widely regarded as one of our finest light tackle sports fish, with many anglers specializing solely in fishing for them.

Mullet can be, and often are, caught in the open sea, but the most prolific venues are usually in and around tidal estuaries. There are three species of mullet in UK waters, the thick-lipped and thin-lipped grey mullet and the golden grey mullet. Each species displays varying degrees of tolerance to brackish water. Golden mullet are generally caught in the open sea, but occasionally venture into the lower reaches of an estuary. The thick-lipped mullet are common in brackish water, and can often be caught well upstream towards fresh water. The thin-lipped mullet are common in both brackish and fresh water well inland from the saline influence of the sea. Hence they are often caught by freshwater anglers.

Mullet start to appear in the south of the UK mainland as soon as the water starts to warm up in the spring, and remain throughout the summer and early autumn. On hot sunny days they are often seen cruising around, sipping at plankton and other particles on the surface in harbours and river channels; sometimes they are mistaken for bass. At times like this mullet can be at their hardest to catch, and it was just this sort of behaviour that resulted in the 'uncatchable' stigma.

The two best pieces of advice I would give the would-be mullet angler are, firstly, to be fully aware that the mullet are an extremely cautious fish by nature, and always exercise extreme stealth when fishing for them. Stomping about along the water line in a bright yellow jacket is certainly not conducive to successful mullet fishing. Secondly, to fish as light as possible. Not only are mullet deterred by heavy tackle, but their excellent sporting potential can only be fully appreciated if caught on tackle allowing them to give a full account of themselves. Pound for pound, mullet are one of our hardest-fighting fish.

A shoal of fine mullet grubbing for food around moored boats.

Groundbaiting (known locally as shirvy in the Channel Islands) is a very important part of the mullet angler's technique. The use of groundbait serves three important functions. Firstly, it attracts the fish, secondly it holds the fish in the required area and, thirdly, it educates the fish into taking with confidence the food item that will eventually be used to tempt them on to the hook. The fact that unusual baits such as bacon rind and chicken skin are used around commercial harbours, where the fish become used to scavenging, proves the point. Let's look at each of these factors in turn.

Mullet have an exceptionally keen sense of smell and can be drawn great distances towards the angler. There is nearly always a flow of water in one direction or another within an estuary, and the current should be fully utilized to send a strong scent signal downstream. Mullet regulars often pre-bait a particular mark for several days before they actually fish, and before very long the timing of the arrival of the mullet can be set by your watch.

Like most sea fish mullet are opportunists, and will switch over to whichever food item is most abundant for the bulk of their feeding. By introducing a supply of hookbait into your groundbait, mullet can soon be duped into confidently feeding on that particular item, greatly improving the angler's chances when it comes to fishing for them.

The groundbait can be made up of more or less anything, but in general a base of bran or bread, with a few mashed fish, some fish oil, perhaps a few handfuls of chopped worms or maggots, some particles such as sweetcorn or small cubes of cheese. The list is never ending; just be sure to include some samples of your hookbait with the groundbait. The best all-round hookbaits are bread, small strips of fish or red meat, cheese and maggots.

The need to fish as lightly as possible cannot be over-emphasized when referring to the mullet. Most specialists use freshwater floatfishing tackle, with lines as light as 4lb BS or even less. Hook sizes should be scaled down accordingly, but sizes 8 and 10 are a good guide. When you see a few feeding fish, avoid the urge to cast straight at them. If the fish are spooked you can forget all chances of catching mullet during that session. Try and trot your bait steadily down towards the fish, or better still draw the fish towards your baited hook using a combination of groundbait and loose feed.

Spinning is another very popular technique for catching mullet, especially the thin-lipped. The best type of spinners are small bar spoons, notably the Mepps types, which need modification before use. Firstly the standard treble hook is removed and replaced with either a single or a pair of single hooks, usually fine wired Aberdeens. These are mounted in tandom using a short length of about 20lb BS nylon, so that they trail behind the revolving spoon.

The hooks are baited with several small live ragworm, usually harbour rag, then cast out and gently retrieved. This is light tackle sport at its finest, a highly visible form of fishing where it is often possible to see the take – one of the most exciting ways of catching the mullet.

Plaice and dabs

So far as the flatfish family are concerned the flounder is the undisputed king of the estuary, but in many estuaries substantial numbers of dabs and plaice can also be caught. There is often a lot of confusion when it comes to identifying these three species of fish, which, with a little practice, need not arise.

Plaice are well known for their bright red and orange spots. Many flounders also have similar markings, but plaice have a series of small bony nodules running around the side of the top pectoral fin near the head, and the red spots are usually far brighter and more distinct than those found on flounders.

Welsh International angler Ivor Smith with a nice mullet, caught at the mouth of the River Rumney near Cardiff.

The author with a lovely plaice caught fishing a baited spoon rig on the drift. The successful bait was lugworm tipped with mussel.

Dabs are the easiest of the lot to identify. At a glance they often appear to be transparent, especially the smaller specimens. The skin of a dab is extremely rough when stroked from the tail towards the head. Another strong identification feature is a distinct curve in the dab's lateral line around the pectoral fin.

Both the plaice and the dab display little tolerance of brackish conditions, and for this reason they are rarely caught in the upper reaches of an estuary, except at times of particularly low rainfall when there is an increase in salinity levels. Both species favour areas with clean sand and gravel to mud, especially where there are beds of seed mussels.

A wide range of baits are successful for catching both species. The dab shows a distinct preference for fish baits, including baits that are seemingly well past their best. One notable bait for dabs is stale black lug, especially if it has been previously frozen.

Plaice respond well to fish baits, but most are caught on worm or peeler crab, including cocktails. Specialist plaice anglers often go to great lengths in preparing elaborate cocktails, usually consisting of worms, various types of shellfish, long thin strips of squid and sandeel – and nearly always a fresh chunk of prime peeler crab.

Both species are found nationwide. Dabs can be caught throughout the year but often they feed most voraciously, and are in their best condition throughout the late summer and autumn. Plaice tend to migrate into deeper water through the coldest months of winter in order to spawn. In the spring they move back inshore and feed ravenously. Big catches are often made at this time, but the condition of the fish after spawning is not good, and all spent fish should be returned.

Like most members of the flatfish family, plaice and dabs respond well to artificial attractors. Brightly coloured spoons are the most widely used, along with different-coloured beads.

Results are also greatly increased if the bait is kept slowly moving, which is usually achieved by fishing on the drift when fishing afloat, or by using a plain bomb-shaped lead from the shore. Bites should be given plenty of time to develop, otherwise the fish will be missed.

Pollack and coalfish

Both the pollack and the coalfish are really fish of the open sea, but they are often common around the mouths of estuaries, and in many of the deeper fjords and sea lochs. Both are very hard-fighting fish on light tackle, and, justifiably, are popular with anglers.

It is normally just the smaller fish of up to about 5lb in weight that are caught inshore, but much bigger specimens can be caught on occasions within estuaries. Vast shoals of small coalfish, known as saithe or billet in the north-east, often enter estuaries, where they are very popular with matchmen and junior anglers.

Pollack show a strong preference for areas where there is clearer water and a

Really a fish of the open sea, pollack can often be caught around the mouth of many estuaries, and often well inland in deeper fjords and sea lochs. This fish was caught on an artificial sandeel, trolled slowly behind the boat.

lot of rocks, or around the piles and wooden supports beneath man-made structures such as piers and pontoons. Coalfish, especially the smaller ones, can often be caught in dirtier water and over cleaner ground, including open beaches.

Both species can be caught with a wide range of methods; light spinning tackle probably provides the most sport. More or less any type of lure will catch these fish, but small spoons and artificial sandeels are amongst the best. For the ultimate in light tackle sport, catching pollack and coalies on a fly rod will take some beating. The best time for catching either species on artificial lures is around dawn and dusk, when the fish seem to feed the hardest and nearest to the surface. Offshore, strings of feathers can be devastatingly effective.

Apart from lures, both species can be caught on a wide range of different baits. A live ragworm fished beneath a float or from a drifting boat, in conjunction with a long trace and a minimum of lead, will often sort out the bigger specimens. Pollack can be caught on static bottom baits, including various types of fish, worms and crab, but respond best to baits fished with a bit of movement. Coalfish, on the other hand, will readily take a range of bottom baits, with previously frozen peeler crab being by far the most successful.

Rays

There are six species of ray that the estuary angler can expect to encounter, with some venues, notably Tralee Bay in Co Kerry in Ireland, capable of producing all six of them in a single session. The thornback ray is by far the commonest with a more or less nationwide distribution. Rod and line captures of the other common species, the small-eyed, spotted, blonde, undulate, and stingray, tend to be far more localized.

Many of the top venues for catching rays are either within, or very near, estuaries, with the Thames Estuary, the Bristol Channel and the Solent topping the list. Although the thornback ray and stingray are quite common in fairly brackish water, the other species tend to prefer far higher salinity levels and appear to dislike heavily coloured water.

For this reason captures of these species are often restricted to the lower reaches of the estuary.

It is a sad fact of angling today that at many venues around the country rays are the only sizeable species of fish that is still reasonably common. Populations of rays do tend to be localized, and as such they are extremely vulnerable to over-fishing, especially by rod and line. Common sense therefore tells us that, with the future of our sport in mind, rays should be returned to the sea as soon as possible after capture, especially the rarer species such as the exquisitely marked undulate ray.

Thornback ray

Also known as 'roker' on the east coast, thornback rays average between 6–10lb in weight, however, fish weighing well into double figures are still common. A true estuary species, the thornback is perfectly at home in shallow brackish water, even if it's the colour of chocolate following heavy rain.

Thornbacks favour a seabed of mud, gravel, flat rock and shingle in preference to fine sand, especially where there are mussel beds. The body colour of this species adapts to blend in with the type of seabed over which the fish has been living. This can cause a certain degree of confusion with novice anglers, who often wrongly suspect they have caught a different species. But, as its name suggests, the thornback is covered with dozens of small sharp thorns, more so than any other species of ray.

The natural diet of the thornback includes more or less anything, and this is reflected by anglers who catch thornbacks on a wide range of baits. The best baits for the species are very fresh fish, especially fillets of mackerel and herring, sandeels, and squid. Crab and ragworm also make excellent baits. When winters are mild, the thornback can be caught all the year round. In most areas the fish migrate offshore into deeper water in late autumn, and return as soon as the water temperature starts to rise at the beginning of spring.

Tony Busby, skipper of top Bristol Channel charter boat *Channel Warrior,* holds a typical thornback ray taken uptiding.

Small-eyed ray

After the thornback, the small-eyed ray, also known as the painted ray, is probably the most common species, although its distribution is restricted to the southwest, especially the waters of the Solent and the Bristol Channel. Small-eyed rays do not have the same tolerance of fresh water that the thornback has, preferring the higher salt content of the open sea. For this reason they are usually encountered in the lower reaches of the estuary, but they will migrate further inland at times of low rainfall. An average small-eyed will weigh between 6lb and 8lb, and double-figure specimens are far from rare.

Small-eyed rays like clean coral sand or shingle, especially systems of sand banks, where they can lie in wait for prey in the gullies on the downtide side of the bank. Sand bars at the mouth of the estuary are often populated by this species. Small-eyeds are perfectly happy in very shallow water, and can often be caught in as little as two or three feet of water or less.

Sandeel is by far the best all-round bait for the small-eyed ray and, surprisingly, frozen sandeels frequently outfish a freshly killed or live eel. Squid, long thin strips of fresh mackerel, herring and peeler crab are also very good baits. The first small-eyed rays start to show about the end of April or early May, and remain inshore until the autumn.

Blonde ray

The blonde ray is the largest of the common species of ray, with many specimens topping 20lb. Blonde rays have the least tolerance of fresh water of all of the rays, and are nearly always caught in very deep, clean water. They favour sandbanks, deep gullies, and a strong run of tide.

Blonde rays are nearly always caught on some sort of fresh fish bait, notably live sandeels when fished on the drift. The most productive marks for the species are in the south and west, especially the outer reaches of the Bristol Channel and the Solent. They are usually caught between May and October.

Spotted ray

The spotted ray is one of the smallest species of rays, rarely topping 6lb in weight. Small blonde rays are often mistaken for large spotted rays. The main difference between the two species is that the spots on the spotted ray tend to be darker and larger than on the blonde, and do not extend right out to the wing tips, as they do on a blonde ray.

The spotted ray is often caught over the same sort of ground as the thornback ray, although they do not normally venture quite as far into brackish water. Small strips of fish, squid and crab are the most consistent baits for the spotted ray, but the physical size of this species dictates that small baits will be the most successful.

Stingray

The stingray is a summer migrant, visiting the warmer waters in the south of the country between the end of May and September. An odd individual can

Stingray are common in many southern estuaries during the summer. A tremendous, hard-fighting species of fish, but keep well clear of the venomous sting located in a sharp spur on the tail.

turn up more or less anywhere, but it is generally the shallow waters of the Thames Estuary, the Solent, the Bristol Channel and Tralee Bay in Ireland that are noted for them. They show a strong liking for warm water emitted by power stations, and many of their haunts will be very near to these warm water outfalls.

Stingrays can be caught in less than a foot of water, and will often follow the tide as it gently floods across tidal mud flats previously warmed by the heat of the sun. They show a distinct preference for murky water. The average stingray probably weighs between 8lb and 20lb, but individuals of 30lb are common and much larger fish are caught most seasons. It is the hardest fighting species of ray, and provides tremendous sport on rod and line.

The most successful baits are ragworm and peeler crab, but many of the largest specimens, 'fluke catches' if the truth were known, are caught on fish baits. As the name suggests, the stingray has a venomous sting located in a barb attached to its tail. Handled with reasonable care it is possible to unhook and return the fish unharmed, but careless handling can result in an excruciatingly painful though rarely fatal sting.

Undulate ray

The undulate ray is the rarest of the six species of ray listed here. Apart from two venues, the Solent and Tralee Bay, it is seldom caught on rod and line. A beautifully marked and easily identified species, the undulate averages around 8–10lb. Invariably caught when targeting other species, various types of fish, ragworm and crab appear to be the most effective baits.

Tackle and tactics for rays

Rays are frequently caught by both shore and boat anglers fishing in and around estuaries. Many of these anglers specialize in ray fishing. Unfortunately, so far as the shore angler is concerned, long casts are usually necessary in order to reach the fish. That said, there are many places where rays can be caught quite close to the beach. At low tide rays invariably drop back into the deeper holes and gullies but as soon as the tide starts flooding they will spread out over the surrounding mudflats and sandbanks. Natural features, such as deeper channels, ledges, mussel beds and sand and shingle banks, are the places to target your baits.

Night fishing is nearly always more productive than fishing during the day. Not only do all species of ray tend to be more active at night, but in shallow, clear water they may only swim to within casting range during the hours of darkness. The most productive technique in many venues is to start fishing at low water on spring tides and then to fish the tide up.

From the shore, a single hook paternoster rig with a fairly long hooklength is the ideal rig. Whenever it is necessary to retrieve fish over deeper ledges or rough ground the pulley rig will be the best choice. In both cases hooklengths should be tied using 50lb BS mono line, which will withstand the grinding from the rays powerful jaws. These jaws are designed to deal with the likes of crabs and mussels so finer breaking strains will stand little chance of holding the fish. There is not normally any need to use wire traces for rays, unless there is a chance of hooking a tope or conger.

Strong hooks are essential. The favourite hook with many top shore anglers is a bronzed Mustad Viking

79515, between 2/0 and 4/0. The majority of rays put up very little fight, but their body shape offers tremendous resistance when retrieving them through the water. It is imperative to use strong tackle, and to ensure that only quality components are used.

When fishing for rays, a big mistake that many anglers make is not leaving bites long enough for the fish to fully take the bait before striking. There used to be a saying that suggested pouring a cup of coffee or lighting a cigarette at the first indication of a ray bite, usually a single nod on the rod tip as the fish settles on top of the bait. In other words give the fish plenty of time before striking. Indeed, it is advisable to wait for the rod tip to start bending over as the fish moves off with the bait before attempting to set the hook.

Offshore, uptiding is nearly always the most efficient method of catching rays, certainly over the shallow water marks so typical of most estuaries. The best boat rig is the simple running leger, again tied with 50lb BS line for the hooklength. Uptiding with fixed leads when the tide is running hard or using plain light leads, at times of little flow, are both effective. In deeper water, slowly trotting the bait back downtide towards the fish can also score heavily. Drifting is rarely successful for rays. The exception is blonde rays, which are often caught when slowly fishing on the drift with a live sandeel.

With the exception of the stingray and small-eyed ray, rays are not particularly active fish. The best approach is to try and locate them, and not wait for them to come to you. The best marks are distinctive sandbanks or gullies, natural food traps where the fish tend to lie and wait for the tide and current to take the food to them. However, a good scent trail may be used to draw fish a reasonable distance towards your baits. There is much to be gained from groundbaiting. An old onion sack filled with mashed fish, bran and other scraps of bait, tied on to the anchor warp often does the trick.

Silver eels

Kids, beginners, matchmen and tope anglers all love silver eels! Long, thin, covered in slime and a bait robber, the silver eel is many things, but above all it is a survivor. For many anglers the silver eel is one of the most important species of fish that can be caught in the estuary.

Amongst other things, the silver eel has one of the most interesting life cycles of all of our sea fish. Silver eels spend most of their lives in fresh and brackish water piling on weight prior to spawning. When the time comes for spawning, it's no short trek down to the sea for this fish. Silver eels spawn many thousands of miles away in the western Atlantic, in an area known as the Sargasso Sea.

The young eels then drift back in the ocean currents, a journey taking several years, eventually entering our estuaries when they measure about 3–4in, at which stage they are known as elvers. Gradually they work their way towards fresh water. They can often be caught in and around estuaries, and they are normally most active between spring and late summer. A few fish remain in fresh water for many years, some specimens topping 10lb in weight, but a typical estuary eel will weigh between 12oz and 2½lb.

Eels are usually eager and greedy feeders and can be caught on a wide range of different baits. Probably the top quickly turn your terminal tackle into a useless mess.

Rigs incorporating long hooklengths are usually the most productive, but these also tend to create the worst tangles. Hook sizes should be between about size 1/0 and 4. Fine wired patterns such as the Aberdeen tend to be the sharpest, and also the easiest to remove from deeply hooked fish.

Good places to locate eels are in and around the main river channels, especially where small side streams or reens enter the estuary. Sewage pipe outlets can be very productive, but anglers should be extremely wary when fishing at such venues, especially if they have any open cuts on their hands.

One of the optimum times to catch eels is following a warm summer day with a flooding tide. Eels will often feed at their best during hot, humid and thundery conditions. A useful tip is quickly to wrap any eels that are caught in an old towel or newspaper. This will prevent the eel tangling your trace into an unusable mess, and make unhooking a lot easier.

Dave Loader, a former Welsh International, with every match angler's favourite. A silver eel caught at Magor in South Wales.

all-round bait is a small chunk of fresh peeler crab. They can also be caught on all types of marine worms, fish, shellfish and even garden worms, where the freshwater influence is strongest or following flooding.

Legering is the standard technique, with single, twin or even three hook paternosters commonly used by anglers who set out to catch them. It is advisable to keep rigs as simple and tangle free as possible, as a squirming eel can very

Smooth hounds

There are two species of smooth hound in Britain, the common smooth hound and the starry smooth hound, which is often a more 'common' capture on rod and line than its close cousin, despite its name. Both are commonest in the south and west and rarely caught north of a line drawn from Anglesey to the Wash. Smooth hounds are one of our hardest fighting sea fish and give a very good account of themselves on balanced tackle, especially when caught in shallow water – when they have been known to jump clear of the water during the fight. They

One of our hardest-fighting sea fish, the smooth hound. Kevin Launder holds a good double-figure specimen, caught from a rough ground mark at Aberthaw in the Bristol Channel.

are of little value as a food fish and consequently all smooth hounds should be returned.

The common smooth hound is a uniform light grey in colour, the starry smooth hound is speckled with small white spots, hence the name. Crab is by far the favoured food item of both species, the flat grinding plates that serve as teeth bare witness to this. The great mystery with smooth hounds is, if they feed mainly on slow moving crabs and

other crustaceans, why do they have such an incredible turn of speed? Both species are abundant inshore during the late spring and summer.

Smooth hounds appear able to tolerate fairly brackish conditions, as well as coloured water, but they are rarely caught upstream near the area of greatest fresh-water influence. They hunt in packs, and when one smooth hound is caught there will nearly always be plenty of others in the near vicinity. Smooth hounds are creatures of habit and if they show in a particular place at a particular state of tide, then it's a fair bet they will be back the next time these conditions coincide.

Good areas to look for smooth hounds are reefs, outcrops of rock, mussel beds or sandbanks, in fact anywhere where there are populations of crabs. Common green shore crabs are probably the mainstay of their diet but over sandbanks they feed heavily on hermit crabs. In some areas smooth hounds are caught on ragworm and squid baits and, very occasionally, on fish.

Afloat, light to medium uptiders are perfect for catching smooth hounds, although a rod with a bit more 'beef' in it may be needed where the tide is running hard. Ashore, one of the most pleasurable methods to catch a smooth hound has got to be on a bass rod or a light beachcaster. Unlike tope, smooth hounds do not have teeth, so wire hook-lengths are not needed, nylon of about 50lb BS is more than adequate.

Tope

The tope is the largest species of fish that an angler is likely to catch within most estuaries. A member of the shark family, tope can be caught in good numbers,

Tope are fairly tolerant of coloured and brackish water but show a preference for more saline and cleaner conditions. Occasionally caught from the shore, it is essentially a boat angler's species, which, when caught on light tackle and in the shallow water environment typically found within an estuary, provides outstanding sport.

In shallow water uptiding is easily the most productive method of catching tope, which are cautious by nature, but in deeper water it may be necessary to revert to traditional downtiding techniques. Being a true shark it has a full and very efficient set of sharp teeth, which would make short work of a standard nylon hooklength. It is therefore necessary to use either wire or heavy duty mono of around 200lb BS.

In addition, it is advisable to use a length of about 10ft of 50lb mono to connect the main hooklength to the main line. This acts as a rubbing length, preventing breakages caused by contact with the topes' rough skin. Obviously a shock leader, if used, will serve the same purpose.

Favourite baits for tope include fresh fillets of fish and livebaits, including flatfish. In recent years sections of silver eels have been responsible for many of the biggest fish caught in the Thames Estuary and the Solent, including record fish (Fig. 30), but for some reason they do not seem to be so successful elsewhere. This has probably got a lot to do with anglers failing to experiment with what, to them, are new baits. The hot spot for shore-caught tope today, is the Isle of Man, and the number one bait there is a small sandeel.

Most tope tend to work the deeper channels and sand banks when feeding within an estuary, but patches of reefs

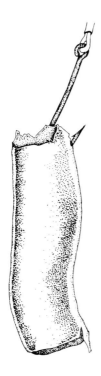

A chunk of freshwater eel has accounted for more specimen tope than any other bait

Fig. 30 Eel section bait for tope.

notably in the Thames Estuary (where the existing British record was caught), the Bristol Channel, the Solent, the Lougher Estuary in west Wales, Tralee Bay in Ireland, as well as many inland seas and lochs along the west coast right up into Scotland.

The first tope start to appear around the end of April and May and, more often than not, these are heavily pregnant females which migrate inshore to drop their pups. Later in the year larger packs of smaller fish, usually the males, start to arrive, attracted by an abundance of food. Their food includes a wide variety of small fish, particularly sandeels, dabs, flounders and silver eels. The tope usually remain throughout the summer, before disappearing almost overnight.

and wrecks are also worth fishing – indeed anywhere where there are quantities of bait-fish. If mackerel are shoaling in the area the fish will often concentrate on feeding in mid-water, and a freelined live mackerel, or a bait fished beneath a float, can work well. Tope respond very well to rubby dubby, which should be used whenever possible.

A big mistake a lot of anglers make when fishing for tope is striking bites (or runs as they are termed) too quickly. Initially tope will pick up a bait and run several yards with it. This is why many anglers fish with their reels in free spool and the ratchet on. Then the tope will pause momentarily, take the bait fully into its mouth, before taking off a second time; this is the time to attempt to set the hook. Waiting too long should also

A typical pack tope of around 20lb, caught from a mark in the Bristol Channel.

be avoided as this can result in the fish swallowing the bait, with obvious risks to the fish. It's all a matter of timing, which can only come with experience.

Tope are purely a sport fish, with little edible value. There is no justification for killing tope; the emphasis should always be to catch and release the fish, causing it a minimum amount of discomfort. To this aim a bronzed hook, such as a Mustad Viking 79515 size 6/0, is ideal, since it can be cut free and left in a deeply hooked fish. Being bronzed, the hook will soon rust and the fish will eject it. Stainless and galvanized hooks should not be used for tope.

Whiting

Whiting are fish of the autumn and winter, when vast shoals often enter estuaries. They can be caught throughout the entire year at some venues but these tend to be smaller fish. Decreasing hours of daylight and falling temperatures make ideal conditions. From the beach, classic whiting conditions are invariably high water during spring tides falling around dusk on a cold and clear, frosty evening.

Afloat, especially when fishing for whiting in coloured water in areas like the Thames Estuary and the Bristol Channel, the fish can, and often do, feed very strongly at any time of the day. A steady run of tide, either the ebb or the flood, depending on the venue, will induce the fish to feed. The first run of a flooding tide is often an excellent time to fish. When the water is clear, fishing at dusk or during darkness can often be more productive than during the daylight. Whiting are fairly tolerant of brackish conditions.

Whiting respond very well to ground-baiting and the scent from several anglers' baits is often more than enough to attract feeding fish. The best baits for whiting are various types of fish: mackerel, herring, sprats, sandeels, even small strips of whiting themselves all work very well. Thin strips of squid and worm baits can also be very effective.

Most rigs work well for whiting but a two or three-hook paternoster is probably as good as any. When the fish are feeding strongly, it is possible to catch them two or three at a time. I have found that short hooklengths of about 4in in length, either fished off booms or swivels trapped on the backbone of the trace, are just as effective and far less prone to tangling than long hooklengths.

Vast shoals of whiting invade many estuaries during the autumn and winter. This fish fell to a bait of king rag tipped with squid, intended for cod.

The wishbone rig is excellent to use for whiting whenever there is a chance of hooking a bonus fish such as a decent cod. The two small hooks, fishing side by side, hold two small baits intended for whiting, but also offer a reasonable chance of securing a firm hook-hold if a larger fish takes either the bait, or, as often happens, a whiting already hooked on one of the hooks.

A lot of anglers use light line for their hooklengths. They probably assume that as the fish are only small there is no need to use stronger breaking strains. But even the smallest whiting has needle sharp teeth (which your fingers will bare testimony to at the end of the session) and these sharp teeth soon damage fine nylon, weakening it considerably. I use 20–30lb BS nylon for my hooklengths, and sometimes heavier.

The ideal whiting hook is a fine wire Aberdeen or any smallish pattern, provided it is needle sharp. However, as with the breaking strain of the hooklength, you should always consider the likelihood of hooking a big cod. For this reason I personally opt for a stronger hook pattern. My current favourites are Mustad's Vikings or Nordic Bends in about size 1 or 1/0.

Another excellent method of catching whiting is using a string of baited mackerel feathers. Each of up to six feathers is tipped with a thin fillet of fish. Always ensure that the hook point is clearly exposed and not masked by the bait. Most sets of mackerel feathers are tied using poor quality hooks; a few minutes with a sharpening stone can pay dividends.

The feathers obviously attract the fish, and the fact that there are so many baits in such a small area can only increase the effectiveness of the scent trail. Hokeye type lures are deadly for whiting and many other species. These have small luminous beads attached to them which I am sure fish find very attractive.

Conversion table

1 in = 2.5 cm
1 ft = 30.4 cm
1 yd = 0.9 metre
1 mile = 1.6 km
1 oz = 28.3 g
1 lb = 0.4 kg
1 ton = 1.016 tonnes
$°F = \dfrac{9 \times °C + 32}{5}$

Index

Page numbers in **bold** refer to the illustrations